Livin Out of Boxes...Letting Go of Bags!

Your Divine Power Awaits You!

ANGELA SIMS-WINFREY

Livin' Out of Boxes…Lettin' Go of Bags!

A Spiritual Journey of Divine Empowerment

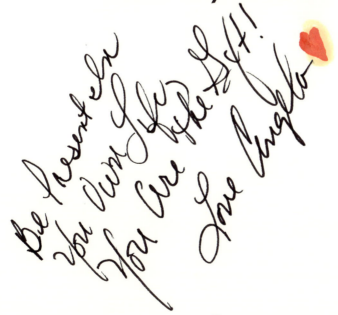

Copyright © 2011 by Angela Sims-Winfrey

All rights reserved.

ISBN: 0615679846
ISBN-13: 9780615679846

I Dedicate this Book to My Son, Brandon, Daughter, Malaikia, My Nieces, Nephews, Young Cousins, their offspring, and all the Sons and Daughters of God who are on a Healing Path of Understanding, Peace, Unconditional Love, Justice, and Divine Living.

Livin Out of Boxes...Letting Go of Bags!

Contents

An Attitude of Gratitude...1

A Message from Angela...4

Prologue: A letter to My Son, Brandon...9

Healing Path One...Divine Principles

A New Birth: A Divine Spirit is Growing...11

Actualizing Faith...14

In God We Trust...18

Take Your Spiritual Gifts Out of Layaway...19

Where is the Love?...24

Healing Path Two...Divine Foundation

Love Just As Much..28

It's Spring Time! What Seeds are You Planting?...32

A Resurrection of Divine Love...33

EGO Trippin'...38

Fear Not! ...42

Superwoman Has Left the Building...46

Family, Friends, Our Lifetime Treasure...51

Healing Path Three....Unpacking Boxes & Bags

Livin' Out of Boxes...59

Job Titles and Job Description: *Divine Work or Distractions...64*

Sistahs Betsy, Camille, Katrina, and Irene

Women Scorned or Pearls of Wisdom?...67

Sticks and Stones...73

Lettin' Go of Bags...75

Broken Wings...78

Healing Path Four...Divine Liberation

Independence?...86

Divine Liberation, The Truth Will Set You Free!...87

Just a Prayer Away, Unconditional Surrender...91

It's Harvest Time!...94

Divine Sunshine!...96

....A Rebirth: A Divine Spirit is Glowing...98

An Attitude of Gratitude!

I am truly in the flow of God's Divine Power. I now understand what it means to Relax and allow God to be in control. What I have learned is that in order to be aligned with God's Greatness you have to let go of "all things" that are not working for you today. When I was insecure and afraid, and my ego's dominance manifest itself in anger, fear, guilt, shame, or disorder, I remembered my Grandma Marybelle's favorite scripture *"COUNT YOUR LIFE BLESSINGS AND NAME THEM ONE BY ONE"*. **I am so Blessed!**

I thank God for stopping me to pay attention to the "cluttered" spaces in my life that was holding the useless things and people. As my space was cleared of "toxic baggage" that was weighing me down, this open space gave me an expanded view of people, blessings, and opportunities that have come to aid my growth in this new life. I was able to see and appreciate the people who have been there all the time. "The clutter, noise, and spam" made it difficult to see or hear them.

I thank God for the "Divinely Timed" situations that made me stop and pay attention to broaden my understanding of the reason why so many of us and our families are experiencing so many challenges at the same time. Many people are moving toward "the truth", the light of our spiritual clarity and there is growing the strength developing in us to "rise above our life challenges". When the **"BRIGHT LIGHTS OF TRUTHS"** shone in my face and caused me to have "temporary" blindness, I thank God for guiding me to a place with the necessary means to "sit still" and reflect on the "totality of my life experiences and "re-tap" into the Spiritual Gifts he blessed me with at birth. I thank God for giving me the opportunity to travel nationally and internationally to expand my skills and relationships that help me to broaden my understanding of the richness of our cultural differences, our universal connectiveness, and our connection as pieces of a puzzle for a Divine Purpose of live and living.

I pay homage to my Spiritual Ancestors whom I have known as family, friends, and work partners who played a blessed role in my existence, wisdom, and guidance that remains in my heart as a constant reminder of love everlasting, forgiveness, strength, and perseverance. To My Daddy, Auntie Lucille, Grandma Marybelle, Nannie V.L, Lil Sister, and Uncle Melvin the memory of your "unconditional love" and spiritual presence in my heart pulled me through the "rough" patches of my "healing path". To the late Rev/Dr. Marshall Truehill, Jr, Joseph "Seyoum Louis, and Jim Hayes, your teachings and Divine Presence in my life is an inspiration for me to pass these bold messages of Faith In Action on to the next generation of leadership to persevere through the fogs of the struggles.

I thank my mother, Effie Mae Brisco-Sims, a Phenomenal Woman and Mother, my First. my first love, my first teacher, my first role model, my first minister, and who raise us to be respectfully strong women to rise above life's adversities. I thank God for my Sisters, Pamela, Antionette, Anna, Paula Michelle, my Sister/Cousin/BFF Paula Marie, Auntie Pauline, and Cousin Alex O'Neal. Although our life paths have us on different branches of same Family Tree, we all have our unique ways of letting each other know that the "home nest" of unconditional love, care, and support is always there. I AM because YOU ARE the mirror reflections of my life growth.

I openly embrace and thank God for the new Love Connection Divinely placed in my life. I am learning to give and receive "love on top" and enjoy a healthy, mature relationship with peace and friendship at it's foundation. I look forward to our relationship growth and spiritual partnership of life, love, and Divine living! "I SEE YOU... BIG HUG!"

ANGELA SIMS-WINFREY

I am so appreciative of the loving, supportive, and encouraging friends and "cheerleaders", the Earth Angels that have been a

part of my life who joined, nudged, pulled, held space, time, taught, coached, mentors, and supported me as I "pushed pass my growing edges" . Creating, keeping focus, staying in a positive space, in preparing my first book for publishing would not have been possible without encouragement and support of my Family, Lifelong Friends, Spiritual Cheerleaders, Mentors, and Work Partners...Keith Sweeney, Paula M. Williams, Nicole Wilson, Chris Ballard, Mike Smith, Balah Muhammad, Mwalimu Johnson, Rev. Dwight Webster, Rev. Lois Dejean, Ifama Arsan, Nana Anoa Nantumbi, Connie P. Jones, Rev. Tyronne Edwards, Barbara Major, Rev. David Billings, Emery Wright, Stephanie Gullioud, Tammi Fleming-White, Petrece Sams-Ibiodun, Berwick" Mahdi" Davenport, Christi Ketchum, Danny Patterson, Tina Green, Kenneth Bowman, Hubert Brandon, Linetta Gilbert, and Latosha Brown, Arkeitha Prince, Carolyn Pittman, Elizabeth Juin, Hope Mabry, and Stacy Wilson, Rhonda J. Miller, Margery Freeman (Editing Consultants), and Tiffanie Smart of Nibs and Reed, LLC (Publishing Consultant), I appreciate you, your Love, and all the TEA (Time, Energy and Attention) you share.

To my St. Thomas-Irish Channel Consortium, Junebug Productions, People's Institute for Survival and Beyond, Gulf Coast Fund, V2V, and Project South Families, you open space for me, mentored, supported, and enabled learning/sharing opportunities for me to divinely share and grow my Spiritual Gifts and Talents for a broader purpose of building a movement for social justice and equity for everyone.

All this love and support is Divine Expressions of God's Greatness. I now know for sure that God's Unconditional Love is my power source and I Am supplied with everything I need to take the next step in my life journey in expressing myself divinely with… **AN ATTITUDE OF GRATITUDE**

Livin Out of Boxes...Letting Go of Bags!

A Message from Angela

By His divine power, God has given us everything we need for living a godly life. We have received all of this by coming to know him, the one who called us to himself by means of his marvelous glory and excellence.
2 Peter 1:3

God is Awesome!

After over 25 years of experiencing and journaling my life experiences, I am here! It was my intention to have my first book be about the insights I gained and the lessons learned in the development of Strong Leaders: Moving from Victims to Victors™. The personal empowerment and leadership development workshops I designed and lead the facilitation to address the internalization of oppression and personal and community disempowerment. However, after many personal "unexpected" life changing experiences and losses, I found myself facing my own "victimhood" fears and internalized messages of oppression that put me in a prolonged state of "emotional traumatic shock". These emotional feelings had me many days feeling alone, insecure, isolated and overwhelmed.

Like many social justice leaders and organizers in the aftermaths of Hurricane Katrina, I immediately went into my organizing mode...finding and reconnecting our people....securing relief resources...participating and organizing meetings and conference calls to actualize strategies to address the human rights violations that occurred in the aftermaths of this country greatest disaster of all times. While in the midst of sharing and hearing the lies and losses exposed by the Divine Power of Hurricane Katrina, I was "passionately motivated" to share and expand my Divine work and purpose of motivating, educating, organizing, and facilitating with "my brothers and sisters" fallen down by "unexpected life" struggles. My organizing power was constantly on! All this while trying to secure my own family, get a little rest, and "ward" off the "Katrinacide" stereotypes that shadowed us wherever we went. Most of these stereotypes were fueled by the media scrolled photos and sound bites that paralyzed people in front of televisions around the world. Once in a while, I would breathe a second and glimpse at the television, hear messages and statements defining us based on wherever their perceptions and opinions gave them comfort. This is when I heard "I was a refugee". I thought I was a born and naturalized citizen of the United States. A refugee is person who has been forced to leave their country in order to escape war, persecution, or natural disaster. When did New Orleans become a country I was forced to leave? This message stayed in my head for many years. But it did not stop me from "doing the work".

I stayed in this mode for at least 3 years; only stopping to make sure my family was ok. When the "Katrina" attention started to die down and the new messages cried for us to "get on with our lives", I slowed down and became more present in my own life. As I settled in my latest "home", I realized that I still had a lot of "unpacked boxes" and "baggage piled up" in my life. When I peeked inside the bags, I realized that I had been carrying around a lot of "unaddressed and unhealed" stuff that accumulated from moving from experience to experience, spaces and places. This "not so hidden" baggage was being revealed daily. Deaths, separations, job loss, house loss, were happening so fast. Constant survival questions like whether to stay or whether to go back. Are we staying too long? Are we leaving too soon? What's best us? What's best for the kids? If our family home is gone, where is home? Adapting to new environments and meeting new people while at the same time trying to hold on to old environments and old friends. Cultures colliding, the past, the present, and the future seem to be merging into one single "time period". Nothing was sure or secure. Multigenerational messages piled on that were destined to be passed on. As I look at my reflection through my daughter's eyes, I was determined that this "way of life" has to stop. Malaikia will not be subject to yet another "generational cycle" of box packing and bag carrying that would surely walk her into the "same shoes" that I was wearing. The shoes that were worn out, weather-beaten" and starting to really hurt. The shoes that her older brother witnessed me walk in. THIS HAS GOT TO STOP NOW! I had to make a decision to live outside of external and "man-made" boxes and let go of the "unhealthy" bags I was carrying. HOW WAS I GOING TO DO THIS?

I had to learn some new spiritual lessons. What I had to learn through this labor of Divine Love was necessary for me to be healthier emotionally and physically, have healthier relationships in my life, and become truly "victorious" in my life, I had to "face my own victimhood fears and internalized messages of oppression". I now know that all the challenges and experiences I have had happen exactly the way they did for me to stop, pay attention, and be prepared for the evolved life God has in store for me. Trust me; I did not "ease" on down the road. I "kicked and screamed" all the way through it. I blamed what I could not explain. My control issues and fears had to be addressed for me to open the door to "my healing path". To get through this I needed to embrace my spiritual power and truly be about growing my spiritual understanding and strength. My inner knowing reminded me of our ancestors and the journey they had taken for us to be release from physical bondage. They did not have a television or cable. To read they had to do it in secret, they did not have att&t, verizon network, email, facebook, apps or metro pcs. What they had was faith and a "deep seeded trust" that God would bring them through. They had no choice but to act on this Faith if they truly wanted to be free. They totally surrendered to God's Will be done. We are here as evidence of the results of that "total surrender". So I am having my first book of *Livin' Out of Boxes...Lettin' Go of Bags!*, as spiritual expression of my life experience, a covenant of my commitment to "push through my growing edges", and the truths revealed to me about myself all of which will be emerged in a "spiritual baptism" of lessons, insights, and test of faith.

My main intention for writing *"Livin' Out of Boxes...Lettin' Go of Bags"*, was to "grow through my personal healing", become more balance, and have an emotionally healthy life, I also wanted to share it with others as an inspiration to get through life challenges by sharing your inspirations and telling your own story". I want to leave a legacy of spiritual empowerment to my love ones and those who I encounter in spiritual linkages to expand out to "all of the God's children". I desire to share the spiritual tools that have guided me through the floods of emotional, physical, and economic despairs. When I was journaling it was to the Divine Power Source of God's Unconditional Love that kept me afloat and rising above the "waves" of lack and limitations. Although it was "not planned", my flow of writing the journal was inspired by the seasons. It just happens that my "deepest valleys" coincided with the seasons. My "unplanned" sabbatical this past year enabled me to pay attention to my "seasonal" emotions and energies. What also kept coming to my mind was a lesson I had learned in my "anti-racism" education and training about holidays being "Holy Days". So as I approach the "Holy Days", I wanted a more internalized understanding of spiritual truths, and how these truths spoke to my life experiences and fueled by strength to persevere.

Being a "pocket book" you can carry it around with you to read to serve as motivational vehicle to tap into and "refuel" your Divine Power source for inner strength. As I was writing *"Livin Out of Boxes...Letting Go of Bags,* I was also "growing" through my healing, Divine Spirit "guided" my writing in sync with what I needed spiritually to pull me through some very "Job" moments. I needed some spiritual tools to absorb and internalized, "real-time" messages for reinforcement on my "new path". This spiritual book of Divine Empowerment is divided into four "healing paths" which were critical in

Livin Out of Boxes...Letting Go of Bags!

"pushing pass my growing edges" and strengthening me through the journey. The 1st Path speaks to the spiritual values and principles with reminders, affirmation, and Divine covenants that proclaim the Omnipotent Power of God in our lives. The 2nd Path reflects and affirms the relationships that "seed and fertilize" the foundation of who we are and teaches us about ourselves and "why I do what I do". This "intense path" informs me about where I have matured in my spiritual and personal growth. The 3rd path takes personal and professional inventory of the boxes and bags that we live in and out of and keep "holding on to" that may be preventing us from our "Divine Destiny". The 4th Path spiritual defines and expresses what and how to live life in Truth for Divine Liberation.

These paths are circular. You may have to repeat a path in order to grow stronger to "counteract" distractions or "reappearing" circumstances. You can read or refer to this book as often as you need to. I would also like to suggest that you scan the chapter titles and see which ones reflect you daily spirit and "real-time" challenges. It can also be a spiritual aid when you feel your "spiritual and emotional energies" are low. Even as I was reviewing through an editorial lens, it affirmed and motivated me to stay on the path of "Divine Healing". I share this book as a personal reflection "marking the steps of my spiritual journey and growth for total surrender in alignment with the Divine Power of God's Unconditional Love and Greatness. Now is time to "live in" the truth and "live outside" of the "man-made" artificial boxes that we have been taught to believe is the "source and supply" of life sustenance. The "foundational integrity" of these man-made institutions and structures has been compromise by greed, deceit, and fear. Now is the time that we "tap" into the Divine Power of our existence and "re-juvenate" a spiritual understanding of who we are and who we were created to be a living, breathing valuable expression of God's Greatness! **Angela**

ANGELA SIMS-WINFREY

Prologue: A Letter to My Son, Brandon!

Dearest Son,

God gave you life and you nurtured mine. You are now what society calls a man. But in my heart you have been for a while. Today on your eighteenth birthday, I give you wings to fly not in the direction of what man wants for you but what God wants for you... How will you know what God wants for you...Stop, listen and know your heart. Move in the path of love and peace aligned with your mind, and God's Holy Spirit within your soul. Be kind and sharing without casting your God-given blessings and talents to swine. Be proud without conceit. Use your God-given talents to the fullest. Stay caring and loving to others as you would want for yourself. Stay connected to your elders for wisdom-those whom are among us and those who are in your heart in spirit. Be a leader, but also learn to follow those who lead with God's loving guidance. Be a teacher and a student. You journey of life lessons and learning are just beginning. Seek out Heroes & Sheroes, as your mentors. Meet obstacles as blessings and lessons; they are not problems but circumstances in life journey to grow you. Closer to God. Brandon, I love you and the joy of my approaching "next generation" (Smile) of motherhood has been made greater by having raised a son like you. When this baby is born you will take on another role...Big Brother. Who will be always watch as a role model. I have no doubt in you Brandon, so do not doubt yourself. You are God's child and my child. My blood flows through you as God's Holy Spirit lives within you. Tap into yourself and always remember I AM, the name o God and what it means.

With Unconditional Love and Understanding,

Mozelle (Momma)

Livin Out of Boxes...Letting Go of Bags!

Healing Path One...Divine Principles

ANGELA SIMS-WINFREY

A New Birth: A Divine Spirit is Growing!

In the womb of my birth, I was nurtured in a warm comforting space,

In this nurturing space I grew bigger and began to outgrow that place

A smothering place I had to get out for survival.

If I stayed too long my tiny being would eventually expire.

So it was time to go and face this new world of whys?

As the walls of the space expanded and contracted,

I was pushed out into a place full of confusion and reaction.

There was a light at the opening that grew brighter and brighter

Fill with mix feelings of anticipation and excitement.

The rhythm we shared in harmony with pulse, spirit, and heart,

Skipped a beat and cause our shared spirit to part.

The warmth change quickly to coldness and chill

Full of wonder, hope, and expectations to fill

Livin Out of Boxes...Letting Go of Bags!

I Am now out of "the space that once protected me,

The space that once snuggled is now rejecting me

Toward an unknown journey to live through daytime and night

With the gift of God's love as fuel for my new flight

A flight full of imposed expectations, mixed messages, influences, and prejudgments.

That pushed all of us into boxes that will smother and ruin us

With choices that limit and narrowly defined

That attempts to shape and mold the same kind.

Saying "Pick a box, any box, if you don't pick one for yourself,

We'll pick one for you!

Boxes full of labels, and stereotypes, which distracts us from our true Identities.

Children of God with an inheritance of unconditional love, abundance, with Divine Amenities!

If you don't follow your desires and the natural flow of your soul

Boxed living is the only life in which your story can be told.

The comforted place we search for every day of the week

It's not in a box, a bag, or the other artificial places we seek.

The places and spaces that we seek are within us,

God's divine love and essence is the only comfort we should trust.

It's is our spirit, our sustenance, it the food to our soul

The only thing we need to live life so purposeful and bold.

It's the thumps of our pulse, the breathe of our spirit

God's love never skips a beat in the rhythm of our heart.

The love of God's Divine grace pulled us out of past struggles

His Divine spirit of mercy forgave our mistakes, errors and fumbles......

Livin Out of Boxes...Letting Go of Bags!

Happy New Year!
Actualizing Faith

Faith is being sure of what you hope for and certain of what you do not see...Hebrews 11:1

Action: to move on an act or goal

Actualizing: to express an act into reality

Reality: to make real; to bring to light Truth

Truth: is eternal. The truth never changes. Truth is consistent, dependable, and born of God's Love. When our consciousness (internal awareness) opens and embraces the belief of Divine (God's) Truth, a greater understanding unfolds. The truth is that our lives are direct reflections of our conscious and subconscious thoughts. The thoughts that dominate our minds manifest our current reality. As long as we breathe the spirit of life, we can choose a different reality by shifting our thoughts to see our needs and desires being fulfilled. This greater understanding opens our hearts and thoughts to a Divine Truth that we have everything we need to receive our life desires. Our existence is the greatest expression of God's Divine Truth.

As we move into a new year we share and express our hopes, wishes, and dreams for ourselves and each other. There is a space in time that we shout out with joy and happiness the beginning of something new. If we can visualize our hopes, wishes, and dreams we can create a "new reality" not only by our words but by our behaviors and actions toward others as well as ourselves. "What we plant, will grow" and "What we reap we have sowed". These are Truths that have been evidenced by our past experiences and current realities.

> ### *The Question Box*
>
> *We make these statements, but have we internalized them? What seeds of hope, wishes, and dreams have we planted for the New Year? What threads we are sewing? What patterns or behaviors that we are expressing that feed its growth? Are they patterns or behaviors grounded in fear, insecurity, limitation, and judgments that fail to thrive? Are these patterns and behaviors nutrients of trust, patience, faith, abundance, and love that prosper? Are we intentional about nurturing our hopes, wishes, and dreams? Or is it just some rhetoric that just "sounds good"? At midnight we shout out into the universe "Happy New Year"? What are we doing to manifest this happiness in our lives and the lives of those we wish well throughout the year?*

The prayers we pray at midnight have already been answered waiting for us to be prepared to receive the blessings. When we express our hopes, wishes, and dreams we are responsible (responding to our ability), capable (have the capacity to do the work to make it happen) and accountable (counting on our ability to see it to fulfillment).

Our word is our bond. We seal our bond by honoring the Truth. Honoring our Truth is our Integrity. Let us start this New Year in true expressions of God's Greatness, and be very intentional, discipline, and diligent in nurturing the seeds we planted at midnight. Let our resolutions (agreements) with ourselves and others be grounded with the integrity with our Divine Foundation intact.

Livin Out of Boxes…Letting Go of Bags!

Divine Covenant

Let's put our wishes, hopes, and dreams by manifesting our Faith into Action. If we do this consistently in relationship with ourselves and others we will realize and witness these wishes, hopes, dreams. So when we ring in the "New Year", the happiness that we shout out will be rooted in a "New Reality" as a testimony of what WE HAVE planted, nurtured, and grown!

My New Year Resolution is...

In God We Trust!

The Lord is My Shepherd, I shall not want. (Psalms 23)

The past few years have been full of life changes, trials, challenges, and test. Test of spiritual strength and faith in God to rise above the challenges. **AND WE ARE STILL STANDING!** I have been both blessed and inspired by your support, love, and patience. It is because of these blessings and mutually expressed desires from all of you seeking to get out of the cycles of lack and limitations, which inspires me to attract Divine Partners. Who are Divine Partners? Those who ready and able to invest time, energy, and attention in really working all that we can now tap into God's storehouse of Divine Living. I am looking "for authentic partners" who are ready to move past fear, have the courage and the will to share with agreements of honor, open hands and hearts. The partners I am seeking to attract are persons who are willing and able to bring their Divine talents and gifts to the table of transformed living. It is Divine Work that will enable, facilitate, and make sure that everyone who comes to the table has a place to sit, eat, and enjoy this beautiful life God has blessed us with.

Let's put together a list that is an expression of our Divine Works (not a resume, God don't need to see another resume or a curriculum vitae - we don't have nothing to prove to anyone but ourselves).

Livin Out of Boxes...Letting Go of Bags!

The Question Box

Who? US and anyone else you know that are seeking to get out of the "cave of discontent". What Spiritual Gifts, talent, resources, networks, creativity, and time do you are "you able" to bring to the "Table of Divine Works"? Why am I doing this? We must leave this vicious cycle of powerlessness, lack, limitation and dissatisfaction.

Divine Covenant

We must "present" this list with a trust in God's Omnipotent power and trust in ourselves to attract those who can be trusted. We must bring accountability (count on our abilities) and our word to do what we say we are able to do. We must bring our responsibility (respond to our ability) and bring accessibility (be accessible to our Divine Partners) by making a covenant with ourselves in authentic Divine Agreements. When? Now! How? Start by working on your Divine List and share it with somebody.

ANGELA SIMS-WINFREY

Take Your Spiritual Gifts Out of Layaway!

Wisdom...Knowledge...Faith...Healing Work...Prophecy...Discernment of Spirit...Multilingual Translation...Teaching...Organizing..

Compassionate Giving...Hope...LOVE!

Spiritual Gifts given to each one of us individually, but it is the Divine Spirit of God that activates all of them in every one of us for "community good"! ...

In Reflection of 1Corinthians12

We all have been given certain "Spiritual Gifts" to address any situations we encounter on our life on earth journey. Do you know your Spiritual Gifts? Is it the Gift of Wisdom, the Gift of Knowledge, the Gift of Faith, the Gift of Healing, the Gift of Hope, the Gift of Prophecy, the gift of Discernment, the Gift of Expression through multi-languages and dialects, or the Gift of Translations and Interpretations. Are you Gifted in teaching or have the Gift of Compassionate Giving. Is it a combination of any of these Divine Gifts? How do you know if you are actualizing these Spiritual Gifts? Are you functioning or performing your work "responsibly" (responding to your inner voice of divine wisdom), or you re-acting to, repeating, making "perceptive" judgments and/or internalizing "unhealthy "paralyzing" cultural or societal noises.

Are you working in your Divine Purpose or working just for institutional or personal gain? Do you really know who or what you are working for? You see, we all have been given Spiritual Gifts. Some of these gifts have been misunderstood, dismissed, exploited, taken for granted, disrespected, or neglected.

Livin Out of Boxes...Letting Go of Bags!

Working for the "common good" (the community's good) has somehow got tossed out of the window, along with integrity and accountability. With all of this "egoic" confusion and distraction going on just to do work, are we "sure" that Divine Work is taking place? Is it just in mission work, charity work, or volunteer service? Even in some of these places of services, without a spiritual guidance and accountability to those who are most impacted by your work, and/or cultural understanding "our helping", can become counterproductive, depleting or disempowering to those we seek "to help". We can be doing "so much unaccountable helping", we can deplete our on energy to the place that we are not effective to anyone including ourselves. Are we giving and assisting freely from our heart or with conditions or expectations of self-gratification? Whatever our true intentions in the "income" of our services will be reflected in its outcome".

Where are you aligned with your Spiritual Gifts? Do you know what they are? Have you covered them up for the sake of trying to get on "the playground"? Have you "just missed" being "run over" by the "rollercoaster of greed"? Are you just sitting on your "butts" being programmed into paralysis by the "sound bites of the media machine? We know what the answer is. We feel it in our guts and in our souls. Some of us are just unable to get off "the rollercoaster". We just have "to jump off", uncover and strengthen our Spiritual Gifts for guidance and Divine directions. The truth is that all "the illusions" and "magic tricks" have been uncovered. The "magical wand is broken. This is our time to get out of the "magician's boxes", and let go of the bags of deceit and lies that we have been holding on so long. We must search out and take the covers of our Spiritual Gifts and use them for the greatest and highest good. Our struggles of today are our "points of power", and we are being prepared for our next place to share these Gifts. It appears in our journey of living, life and seeking financial security, we have "displaced our Spiritual Way" in exchange for an unhealthy codependence in the "institutional wilderness". This prolong state of living has rendered as "perpetual victims" and spend our days complaining "in the caves and kitchens" of discontent. We must use all our Spiritual Gifts to become walking, talking Divine Expressions of God's Greatness.

We just need to remove ourselves away from our egoic fears, other's fears, negative societal noises, and tap into our Divine Power Source. How do we get away from "these fears and noises"? We must start by getting out of our head that our identities are permanently tied to our circumstance or man-made institutions. Our circumstances or only "temporary stops" along our life's journey and the institutions are where we work or "do" service. These jobs are not our destiny; they are only steps on the way toward our Divine Purpose. Remember our Spiritual Gifts are to work for the common good. Common good is defined as "good work" shared and beneficial for all (or most) members of a given "community"; not what's "good or beneficial" for one person or one group of people. Institutions don't grow themselves, people grow them. When our "work" fails to thrive, grow, or cease to be our "livelihood", we have to pull up our roots and replant them in more fertile ground. It is where our "divine work" is able to be refreshed for an evolved journey. We also must be truthful to ourselves and act on these truths, that "the place" we walked into is not the same one we or being walked out of. It was change by its experience with us and we were "changed" by our experience working within it.

Just dust yourself off, "thank them" for the experiences, the valuable lessons gained and move forward. Know for sure that the new vehicle we are driving is divinely-powered and plugged into God's Power Source, full of Grace, Mercy, Sustenance, and Unconditional Love. This is the fuel and food for our soul and it will never run out of energy as long as we stay plugged in. Knowing and growing our spiritual gifts will transformed us to become evolved expressions of God's Greatness.

Livin Out of Boxes...Letting Go of Bags!

Divine Covenant

Let us affirm to use wisely our TEA (Time, Energy, and Attention), to become "mo better" in actualizing our spiritual gifts. Again, I ask the question, do you know what your spiritual gifts are? Knowing is the first step to "being". Being about it moves spiritual gifts into doing Divine Works. The only work that is built to last is Divine Works! Let us stop putting a "little bit" at a time on developing our Spiritual Gifts. The strength of our "spiritual future" is relying on our ability to respond with spiritual maturity" to life changes. Let us take our Spiritual Gifts out of "lay-a-way's" artificial storage bags and boxes. Open them up in the breath of our Divine Spirit and allow God's activation of there release to flow!

ANGELA SIMS-WINFREY

To each is given the manifestation of the Spirit for the

common good

1 Corinthians 12:7

Livin Out of Boxes...Letting Go of Bags!

Where is the Love?

Today and yesterday feels the same.

Loss, separation, and grief fuel the pain.

Families together, separated, and spread out.

From east to west, north to south.

A never ending story that keeps going on, and on, and on

Make it impossible for your strength to stay strong

Hurricane Katrina came to cleanse away the mask

Exposing the abuse and neglect of the cast.

A cast of actors pretending to care

Faking out support and putting on airs

Where is the love that once flowed through hearts?

That kept our human connections and shone light in the dark.

The love is still there embedded in debris

Waiting for us to let it flow free

Get the noise out your ear

This fuels the rhetoric of fear.

The love is not somewhere

It is someone and that someone is **YOU!**

ANGELA SIMS-WINFREY

YOU are the space that holds the embedded heart

YOU are the candle that shines through the dark.

Hold your head high

Let **YOUR** love shine

Shout out **YOU OWN HEALING STORY**

For grace and its glory.

Shout out **YOUR OWN STORY!**

Over the sound bites and fluff

Let the world know we are not talking a political recovery

But the recovery of human hearts.

Make a love connection wherever **YOU** are

In your family and community…both near and far.

So you never have a question

IT'S WHEREVER YOU ARE!

What's Your Story?

Livin Out of Boxes...Letting Go of Bags!

Healing Path Two...Divine Foundation

Agape Love!

The Gift of Love___ is wherever we are...its in everyone we meet...a Gift that keeps on giving___Love is patient...Love is kind...Love never fails...and now Faith, Hope ,and Love Abide...out of all three the greatest of these is Love.

1Corinthians13

Livin Out of Boxes...Letting Go of Bags!

"Love Just As Much"

> ### *The Question Box*
>
> *Have you ever thought about how much you love somebody or how much someone loves you? Should you seek or be with someone because "you think" they love you more than you love them. Have you stayed in a relationship out of fear that you are "not worthy" or will not be able to find true love? Have you sought after relationships or stayed in relationships that you felt or feel they are better than you and will make you better or look better? Are you are just playing with love and hoping by the "roll of the dice" that one day you will get lucky? Have you prayed for someone to love you more and got exactly what you prayed for?*

We pray for that special one too love. Be "careful" of what you pray for...your prayers will be answered, however, it may not show up looking like you expected. When you love someone more than or they love you more it will reflected back to you with all the "trappings"- insecurities, self doubt, worth, loneliness in the center of the relationship. When you play with love, you will eventually get "played". Whatever you are putting the most attention on will be what will grow inside the relationship. Eventually somebody in the relationship will want more than the other can give and it will lead to more insecurity and more unfulfilled expectations, and more unhappiness. The relationship will exist with many bouts of sadness and unhappiness. No matter what side of this relationship you are on, the knife cuts the same and somebody if not both will be hurt there will be disappointment. There will be guilt. There will be resentment and there will be pain. Sometimes we "unconsciously" think we love someone more than they love us. But is it them we really love or we are drawn to the person because of a conscious or unconscious desire for something they have or can give us?

There are some people (you know who you are) who "consciously" search for someone and pretend to love just to get something from the other person. Most of the time what they are looking for someone to give them they should be getting for themselves. Once they get what they want or find out they are not going to get what they desired, they move on without even thinking about the consequences of their actions or the injuries cause due to their "love under pretense". There are some people who go into "unrequited" love in full knowledge that this relationship will not "reciprocate" your love relationship needs. This "love more than" or "love less than" will eventually be revealed and one or both people involved will find themselves with "more" disappointments and relationship injuries and eventually the "perpetrator" will have to pay in the Divine Order of reciprocity.

There are relationships that are here for a specific reason or purpose. These types of relationships usually come when we need assistance, rescuing, "rebound band aids", or to assist us through our "growing pains". These relationships are sometimes nurturing and supportive. However, once the person is rescued, saved, on there feet or out of harm's way; the rescuer is no longer needed. The reason or purpose that has been accomplished and the relationship just ends. The person being rescued might stay on out of guilt and prolong the inevitable---the relationship's end. Both the rescuer or the rescued can feel the relationship was more than serving a purpose, they may hold on pass the point of pain in hopes that the person will need rescuing again or keep creating "crisis" that keeps the relationship in a never ending cycle of "unhealthy co-dependency. If both people are honest with themselves about why they were in the relationship they will just move on. Sometimes we know when our relationships are not thriving but we hang on for comfort sake. However none of these relationships of "more than", "less than", or "just enough" can be sustained. If we decide to stay in them whether physically, mentally, or emotionally, we choose a life of unhappiness and discontent. Staying in these types of relationships can also block or take up space physically, mentally or emotionally needed for more fulfilling relationship. This includes the relationship you must have with yourself. If the relationship was meant to last and you really love someone, you will love them enough to let them go. They may grow or realize they love you "just as much" and return. If they do not return, it will open up a space for another who may be the one who is able to love "just as much".

Don't get me wrong all relationships experiences stem from choices and decisions we have made. Whether good, bad or ugly, all relationships come into our lives not to teach us about the other person, but to tell us something about ourselves. It is up to us to pay attention to who we are, what we want, what we do, and who we seek, to fulfill our heart's desire with True Love spiritually grounded in honesty and truth.

What we are seeking is "unconditional love". We know how it feels is because we have experienced it before when we have had pure hearts. We usually give and receive unconditional love from our children, other children, really close friends, and/or our pets. We know their hearts are pure because they connect with the purest of our hearts. We also know how unconditional love feels because we know that unconditional love is the kind of Love God gives us.

God loves us through our good selves, our bad selves, and our "mess ups" and mistakes. God loves us when we do not love ourselves enough. God loves us without expectations, disappointments, judgments, without proof or conditions.

We expect unconditional love from others and don't have this kind of love for ourselves. As we grow older it seems like our view of love gets distorted, influenced by external factors, and societal views. The purity seems to leave our heart and get replaced by distrust, fear, hurt and pain. When we do express love its painful shadows follows us, expressing it with conditions on whom, what, and how we are going to give, receive, or share it.

We become stingy with sharing our love, and don't understand why we are not getting the love we desire. We place expectations on our love ones and if unfulfilled we are disappointed. Disappointment leads to judgment. Judgments lead to penalties and more conditions. These penalties and conditions on how we share love "boomerangs" right back to us and we end up in a perpetual cycle of unhappiness seeking "true love".

True Love will begin to show up in our lives when we begin to "nurture and grow" unconditional love in ourselves. Start by growing a "loving and caring friendship" with yourself. This will open the door for you to have the capacity to draw and receive love honestly, trustfully, and unconditionally. Whatever the relationship is, what it becomes, or how it gets defined, it will be for a lifetime because "true love stays in your thoughts, heart, and spirit forever.

How will we know when we have true love? You will know when you have nothing to give but love. You will know you have true love when you give from your heart freely, without conditions. You know when you have true love when you don't have to do anything or prove anything. You just have to show up and "Be and Do You".

You will know you have true love when you become "True Love" because **YOU ARE TRUE LOVE!**

You are a Divine Expression of God's unconditional love and greatness.

So now when you say your prayers, do not pray for someone loving you more, or just enough to fill your ego through insecurities, fears, and temporary weaknesses. Pray for "just as much love" as you are willing and able to give. Pray for "just as much love" as God loves you, "Unconditionally".

Livin Out of Boxes...Letting Go of Bags!

It's Springtime! What Seeds Are You Planting?

Are you planting seeds of fear, doubt, and discontent?

Or seeds of faith, trust, and joy?

What plants will it bear? Are plants grown with forgiveness, love, peace, and harmony? Or plants of unforgiveness, hate, anger, or chaos?

What soil are you using or placing the seeds in?

Is it full of "old fertilizer" that will smother it growth or fresh fertilizer made with nutrients of care, kindness, and love?

Are you tending to it everyday? Pulling up the weeds? Are you are letting them get overgrown? Or you are waiting for someone else to tend to it?

Are you talking to your plants with uplifting words of more "yes you will or can", than no you can't or won't.

God says be fruitful and multiply? Are you being fruitful or are you just "eatin" off everyone else's fruit? What fruit will your plant bear? What will be multiplied?

Are you working in your garden by yourself or building relationships with others to multiply more fruit? Will you share it with others or will you "hoard" it just for yourself?

What "You" reap is what you will sow. What Seeds you plant will surely Grow.

Our life experience makes us know for sure...

That we have been in this place before!

ANGELA SIMS-WINFREY

A Resurrection of Divine Love

As a "cradle" catholic my momma made sure that we went to church, catechism, and received all of our sacraments. I even "rushed" in the sacrament of marriage before I was ready to be married. As long as I can remember, I was always questioning things I felt didn't make sense. As a little girl, I was always told "I talked too much and asked too many questions". These are the times when "my mouth" would get me in trouble. You were not suppose to have an opinion or question anything about church. You just did exactly what you were told to do. I was so "unimpressed" with catechism; I would do whatever it took to "skip" out of going. What got my attention was when I was preparing for my sacraments starting with my 1st Communion. I excited about wearing a beautiful white dress and veil. I was excited to be a part of the "ritual" of preparing to "officially taste" the bread and drink some wine." I say "officially" because I would "sneak" in line when my mom did not go to the same mass we went to, and "pretend" that I had already had my 1st Communion. (This would come back to me later on in life, when my son, would come home from college and attempt to have communion. But that is another story.) What I did not realize was that before I could take my 1st Communion I had to "do" my 1st Confession. "You mean I have to go in "that box" and tell "that man" all the "bad things I had done including skipping catechism"? Couldn't I just tell God directly? This was my earliest memory of what a "gatekeeper" was. My "mouth" again had gotten me in trouble. So I surrendered, went in "the box" and told "some of my sins". I was not going to tell him everything. I just wanted so badly to "take my 1st Communion". This sacrament was the most significant spiritual memory for me because this is when I begin to learn what my relationship was to Jesus, the Christ and the role of God in my life. This is where I learned that the Son of God, **JESUS DIED SO WE CAN LIVE**.

As a child growing into adulthood, my Lenten and Easter season rituals were to give up something I really enjoy eating (I always gave up chocolate candy), participating in Palm Sunday services (when we got our blessed palms), Good Friday when we couldn't eat meat (the day of our fish, potato salad, and green peas supper) and of course we look forward to the "main event", Easter Sunday. Early Sunday morning we would get dress in our new dresses, a hat, shoes, with a matching purse. The aroma of food cooking "excited" our noses and stomachs. We look forward to coming home from church to our "big supper" and indulge in all the "stuff we gave up for lent". All dressed up in our "Easter Parade" outfits we would share in "the body of Christ", and sing ...*We are one in the Spirit, we are one in the of Lord...* We would have a "momentary interruption" of what this the Easter Week was really about. You mean we are "one" with Jesus? Taking of "holy communion" became a ritual that made me feel the most connected to God.

As I grew older in adult life experiences, my "growing pain" challenges pushed me into "wanting" to be connected to God more than just communion or Easter season rituals. I needed to be connected in some deeper more lasting ways. So I begin to pay attention to the other messages of how we can be more connected to God. Yes, to "do service". So my journey of "intentional "doing service" and community work evolved. This journey took me in many spaces and places. I worked with people from all ages, races, and walks of life locally, regionally, nationally and internationally. But somehow, the more people and places I experienced evoke more challenging circumstances and understandings of why I was not feeling good about who Angela was in the midst of "the doing". "Doing" good community work and service made me feel better about "helping people". However, because of my "disguised" and "unhealed" low self value and self-worth, "my doing" morphed into "an addiction of people-pleasing" I stop doing it "to grow" my relationship to God, and starting "doing service" to prove my worthiness to people. Something was missing.....
When I found out I was pregnant at 39 years old, I realized that God had given me another opportunity through birthing another "blessing of life" to pay attention to all that I was "consuming" that would prevent a healthy birth outcome, physically, mentally and spiritually. Malaikia being born at the same time my son, Brandon was becoming a man was truly a transformative period of my life. Throughout my pregnancy of my daughter, I came face to face with all the labor pains and

joys of my life. She pushed her way into existence, just as I was "pushing" my way into moving from just existing, doing, to growing into the woman I was destined to be. **THIS WAS MY RESURRECTION OF DIVINE LOVE. THIS WAS MY 2nd COMING –OUT.** This journey opened up a passageway for a more truthful spiritual awakening connection with God". I was determined to have a better understanding of how in touch and in tune I was in the frequency of the being in "Communion" with God inside of me.

What I learned is that we are all connected to God by the power of a Divine Spirit within us, through us, around us, that connects us. That God is not just in our places of worship. I was learning that I needed to absorb "the truths" of my existence beyond what I could see, hear, touch, or taste. I had to develop an "inner sense" that I need to learn how to trust. In my "season" of intentional spiritual growing, I approached the Lenten Season differently this past year. I begin to study and develop a deeper understanding of the sacrifices I made during lent. My Divine Understanding led me to "fast from the toxic spirit and energies" I consumed everyday that was blocking my spiritual passageways from getting closer to God. My new lessons were revealing to me that the Lenten and Easter season were more than about sacrificing the things we really like, going through Passover rituals, and preparing our "external look" for Easter Sunday.

I now understood that our fasting and rituals must be for a Divine Understanding of how we are "One in the Spirit of God" by understanding the life and journey of the Son he put here on Earth as a guide to our communion. Our spiritual development and rituals must go beyond Lent, Passover, Good Friday, and Resurrection Sunday. We must take time for a spiritual retreat to "detoxify" from negative intrusions of our mind, body, and spirit every day, every hour, and every second. We must stop "speeching" about what God is in our lives and start being "living expressions" of God's Greatness. It would be a beautiful thing on Easter Sunday to celebrate that the "toxic spirits and energies that we have "inhaled" are no longer a part of our "living temples". We celebrate how we were evolving into living and being like God's Greatest Expression…Jesus, the Christ. It is not WWJD? It is about what "You and I" are being and doing. It does not matter how little or large our blessings. Everyone or anyone we meet today is the least of our Brothers and Sisters! It is not up to us to be the judge of who is "the least". Whomever we judge will "boomerang" right up in our face. The question now becomes WAIB/D? (What Am I Being and Doing).

Many of us have been socialized to see everything and everybody from an external lens. We are waiting on the "2nd Coming" for something or someone from the outside of to come for us to see with our physical eyes the proof that "He has arrived". He is already here in all of us. We must pay attention to when we are going through "these test of faith" valleys; these valleys give us the opportunity to grow our spiritual strength through "blessed lessons". They are the "test" of our Faith, which we don't have to get an "A" in. We just have to learn the lesson and pass the test. We are being tested on our walk of life not just our talk and "squawk" of life.

In my "resurrected" learning, I have learned how to address my people-pleasing addictions by "healing" my sense of self-value and self worth. I had to be just as much as a "cheerful receiver" as I was a "cheerful" giver. I had to truly believe that I am worthy of the blessings I receive. I am learning that we as givers must give from a "place of Love and Compassion". What we share should not be with conditions. We should give cheerfully from the heart.

We can't give from this deep place unless we become Love and Loving! We cannot be compassionate unless we "listen" with our heart, not our EGO (Easing God Out). EGO will only do what it is supposed to do "look out for itself, protect itself, and hold on for itself (because there "may not" be enough). How can there not be enough in the "Kingdom of God". Many of us are experiencing these "valley" because we have "been to the mountaintop". We would not know "the bottom" if we had not experienced some aspect of "Joy" somewhere in our life. We go through challenging circumstances as a reminder or deeper understanding of what we are here to do. Everyone and everything that is in our lives today are supposed to be here to teach us about our selves so that we can "grow into our Divine Purpose. You see as little children, we do what we are told, we were told that we should not speak without permission; we could not dare "questions" those things that did not make sense to us or made adults "uncomfortable". However, we are no longer children. We are adults who have a responsibility to nurture and raise our children in honesty and truth about their "common unity" with God.

The Question Box

What if the 2nd Coming of Jesus, the Christ is already here? We may have just walked over him/her in the street, looked him/her in the face, judged him/her, dismissed him/her, or expressed hatred or distained toward him/her. Are you sure you haven't encountered the 2nd Coming of Jesus already? Have you look in the mirror and look at yourself in the face, judge yourself, dismissed yourself, expressed self-doubt about yourself or hated yourself? Are you ready to make the "common" union with yourself as a Child of God as the 2nd Coming? Is your spiritual passageway "free" of debris? Are you tapping into the Divine Power within yourself to become a living example of God's Love and Greatness?

It's Time to Grow Up!

"When I was a child, I spoke like a child, I thought like a child, I reasoned like a child; when I became an adult, I put away childish ways. We see through a dim reflection when we are children and as we mature we come face to face with a clearer reflection. It's only when we mature we will begin to understand and know our wholeness....1Corinthians 13:11-12

Livin Out of Boxes...Letting Go of Bags!

Ego Trippin'

Struggling with "Ego (Easing God Out)" has been one of my biggest challenges because I spend most of my time "living" in my head analyzing everything through the emotions that attach itself to my ego. When I am confronted with an "unknown life challenge" which "I" am unable to control, I feel insecure and my ego takes over. Ego start holding onto any person, place or thing that "I" think will secure me. Whenever we are insecure we function out of FEAR (False Expectations Appearing Real). Let me be clear Ego has a healthy place and purpose in the Divine space of our being when it is aligned within the substance of Spirit. However, when it is functioning in a dominant role it becomes mis-aligned it seeks "separation" and "isolation" for the sole purpose "self survival". This "top heavy" existence causes the "whole self" to become "off balanced". Being "off-balanced" cause insecurity and sooner or later we will "stumble and fall". You see when our ego is functioning as a "healthy part" of our "being" its key purpose "serves" as a "warning" when "our self" is being threatened. Warnings can be good when it prevents us from moving into a direction "too quickly" that will harm us. However when we begin to function with "alarms" being a way of life, we are in a constant state of anxiety and obsessive need to control everything and everyone around us.

Our "anxious ego "latches" on to things and people under an erroneous illusion that these people, places, or things will give us an identity and make us whole again. Ego "latches" onto past pains to nurture its growth in our "present state".

"WE WERE BORN WITH AN IDENTITY, WE NEVER LOSS OUR WHOLENESS! IT HAS ALWAYS BEEN THERE! THERE IS NOT ENOUGH SPACE IN THE PRESENT TO HOLD ALL THE PAINS OF THE PAST. OUR POINTS OF DIVINE POWER IS IN THE PRESENT!"

Our EGO will try "to stumble" our Faith". When you are insecure and afraid, your ego's dominance manifests itself in anger, fear, guilt, shame, or disorder. Living through the emotions of our ego "blinds us" to the truths we need to be present in "our today's" realities and "paralyzes us from moving forward into the directions of our Divine purpose and destiny. When we are driven by ego, we forget about all the other energies of our being that are necessary for a whole life of living. When the ego "warning light" stays on" we are constantly being signaled that something is wrong or broken with us. You see the warning light does not show the source of the problem or repair the problem. It only signals there is a problem. Without checking in with the other "signals" of our body, and the soul of our spirit, the source of the "discomfort" can never be diagnosed, fine tuned, or repaired. When Ego reacts to a circumstance under the state of insecurity it can "short-circuit" and malfunction. When ego is seeking security it will feed off and use any person, place, or thing to expand its dominance and control.

"THE EGO MUST BE PUT IN CHECK AND BALANCED BACK INTO ALIGNMENT!"

When the "blinded signal light of the ego stays on" all doors of truth become doors of fear and doubt. This "triggers" more egoic fears and if we are not "conscious" and become witnesses of it instead of "passengers" of "its trip" the ego sets "I- self" into a protective mode and view anything "that moves" as a threat. This causes us to protect and defend "our self" from any "perceived attacker". On this "ego trip" we feel shock, tense, afraid, depressed, frustrated, and angry. This "unacknowledged" anger turns to "road rage". Once in this state of "blinded road rage" we passively and/or aggressively attack anyone that we perceive is in way. Passively, we take shelter in our thoughts as a "comfort zone" and participate "covertly" in any "scheme" that "gets back" on those we assumed as cause us injury. Aggressively, we vent our frustrations in a "blind rage" because we limit our thoughts to feeling "boxed in" and "we have to fight our way out of this congested and smothering space".

All the while we are on this "ego trip" we ignore any relationships of our "whole self" or avoid any experiences that are necessary for our healing for long-term movement and growth. Yes, while the ego rejuvenates "our self" with emotional fuel, it may allow short-term relief to "band aid" the injury or wound. However when there is any attempt to connect to our Divine Power Source for long-term healing it reacts with "violent" resistance. When the ego is constantly on, it blocks our view of the "bigger picture" of our Divine Purpose and its connection to the God's Divine Plan, Guidance, and "Will Be Done" in the fulfillment of our purpose.

If we stay keep U-Turning" and picking up pains of the past, we become "victims" of the Ego driving "around and around" on the highway of despair. When ego (easing God out) becomes the primary driver of our life and living trip, we lose the very essence of our "true identity" and "get mis-aligned" in the relationships between our mind, body, and Divine Spirit.

"Balanced alignment" evolves our consciousness and clears a path for purposeful living. It brings out the best of who we are here to be and "the best" of who we are attracts "the best" of what we need. Our "out of sync" ego attracts like relationships to us that keeps us in a perpetual state of frustration and unhappiness.

We must not be afraid to take the Divine Highway of Truth to reach the "well lit" roads of peace, joy, and happiness. By tapping in the Divine Power Source within, we stay connected to God's storehouse of abundance and have an endless supply of fuel and energy for our Divine Journey. That is why we must be just as resistance to allowing the trigger of "egoic alarms" to take over and stay "tuned up" and plugged into to our Divine Power Source to rise above the challenges of our life and living journey.

"So let the ego's purpose be "the alarm" it is meant to be

That direct us to the Truth we "today" must see.

To divinely fulfill a destiny of life and living so joyfully real!

A trip of a lifetime on God's Super Highway of Love, Abundance,

And Divine Prosperity!

Livin Out of Boxes...Letting Go of Bags!

Fear Not!

The Question Box

Are you able to "handle the Truth"? Are you afraid that if you express the truth about who we are out loud you may have to "be about it"? Are we afraid that once we step out on Faith, the journey will get harder?

IT WILL! However, once you pass the test of Faith, your blessings will be more illuminated. Your greatest test will come once you make a commitment to live in "the Light both inside and out.

You will go through periods of "egoic" suffering as Job. During these periods you will be forced to reflect on the meaning of suffering, how to maintain your integrity and "stay steadfast" in your Faith. The spiritual prayers of Psalms and "wisdom pearls" of Proverbs are useful guides through these periods. We are all here to be a Divine Expression of God's greatness.

This is not about the "external noises" that societal judgments and fear imposes on everyone. It's not about sexual orientation, or whether "who should be married to whom". It about the Feminine/Masculine energies of Love everyone has within that "draw" human beings together regardless of outer appearances.

> ### *The Question Box*
>
> *What if we surrender "our ego" and accept that our Divine purpose is simply to evidence and express Truth through our God given gifts, talents, and skills by using the language of the heart? What if we have always had the key but we are afraid to use it because once we cross the threshold of Floor #13 we may have to stop complaining, let go of our not so comfort zone and really live? Why are we so afraid of the truth of our life existence? What if God's greatest expression of Life has been kept away because of the fear of the authentic power of masculine and feminine energy, the union of the opposites, the yin/yang?*

One lie we have been led to believe is that as masculine and feminine love can exist without each other. When the fact is a woman cannot be created without something from a man. You can't make a man without something from a woman. Life can't continue without both. The other "big myth" is the "rugged individual". It is that myth that has propelled us into the society we have today that expresses that "I can do it by myself", I don't need "nobody".

When the truth is we were created as social beings that come into this world as a result of social connections and intimate relationships. As human beings we need each other. Our very essence of survival depends on us being in relationship with each other. The "rugged and strong individual" is not the person who can do it all by themselves, but the person who is "emotionally strong" enough to be vulnerable and work through fears and challenges of all complicated relationships we encounter in our journey of life. Relationships are here to assist in our "growth spurts". They tell us more about who we are, where we are, how we got here, and what we are here to do. No one has done "no thing" by themselves. There has always been a Divine Power protecting us and guiding our way. And if we stop, and count our blessings "one by one", we can remember "that certain someone" who opened a door for us. We have to stop distancing ourselves and isolating ourselves out of fear. We have to stop letting our "egos" and its self protective messages defined our success or failures. We have allowed our fears to be exploited and our organic nature to be tampered with and separate us politically, physically, mentally and spiritually. Our masculine/feminine energy flow must exist in balance for the continuation of the human race.

The societal, economic, and political "pressure cookers" of today are pushing us to go beyond the basics senses of what we see, what we hear, what we feel, what we taste, and what we think. We are being pushed (some of us with grave resistance) to become "multisensory and more in tuned with our "inner spirit for clarity of our life circumstances and purpose. We allow our Ego to use our limited senses to make judgments of who we think people should be, act, and live. We have been physically altered through scientific and environmental interference. We have been mentally impaired through repetitive lies and socialized messages and media "sound bites" of strengths and weaknesses. We have been disempowered spiritually through "his"torical and religious omission of the true roles of key players and principles. We have been "terrorized" by myths, taboos, and superstitions that serve no purpose than to paralyze us into complacency.

To advance socially we have been conditioned to "playing political games" for the sole purpose of obtaining and maintaining "an illusion of power". Until we are still, recognize, reconcile, respect in harmony all the powerful energies within us, and actualize these energies outside for the highest level of good, we will always be in conflict with Divine Order. Everything in and around us will continue in drama and chaos.

Our Divine Spirit is calling on us to pay attention and become conscious of the imbalances in our lives. We must stop putting "band aids" on the open wounds manifested by fear. We must begin to add Truth to our lives, subtract what is not useful for us today, multiply our God-given fruits, and share and express God's unconditional love in relationship with ourselves and in communion with others.

We have to "be willing to bring our whole selves "through" our self-imposed threshold of fear. The 2nd Coming is already here, waiting for us to walk out of the cave of discontent and complacency and get off on Floor #13. It's time to "grow up" and grow into our "Divine Greatness". There is no place for mediocrity, not enough, just enough or "just hanging". It is time that we stop and be intentional about what legacy we are leaving for the next generation to pick up. We all have it in us to leave a difference Legacy...A Legacy of Truth, Life, and One Love!

Fear not, for I have redeemed you;
I have called you by name, you are mine.
When you pass through the waters, I will be with you;
and through the rivers, they shall not overwhelm you;
when you walk through fire you shall not be burned,
and the flame shall not consume you.

—Isaiah 43:1-2

Livin Out of Boxes...Letting Go of Bags!

Superwoman Has Left the Building!

As we were growing up, we would hear messages about our "brokenness" because we lived in homes without both parent or our parents got a divorced. It did not matter what led to this family divide. According to external societal noises we were broken, dysfunctional, or "just wrong". Maybe the family divisions happen due to no longer tolerating the arguments, dysfunctions, the abuse, or trying to salvage some pieces of the family's wholeness. To the outside world it did not matter the reasons. What mattered was what "the outsiders" thought, assumed or just "made up". Our mothers became "single moms" doing what was necessary to keep holding up all ends of the family and home. In some two parent homes some mothers keep up appearances that "everything is fine". Keeping dysfunctions a secret make their day to day existence "pure hell". They stay in these unhealthy situations sometimes for the "sake of the children", not to be seen as failures or lose their social status as being "happily married" What ever the reason Supermom emerged.

Supermom has to be both a caring and nurturing as a mother, as well as tough and hardworking. Supermom became the instant the provider, the protector, the catch all to all of the families trials and tribulations. She has to be the "fixer" of every problem. She just has to be in control or else she will be uncovered as "broken". Who she was as a complete woman became a miniscule aspect of her being. Once Supermom slathers on her red lipstick, put one her badge and cape, her womanhood takes a back seat to everything. Supermom became her identity. This became her internal and external role in life. If she dare attempt to bring out any display of her being as a woman, she is judged "unfit" or made to feel guilty, netting a penalty of ostracism or isolation.

To keep the title of Supermom, she had to do it all. Expectations and disappointments were greater. Any mistake or bad decisions she made were magnified. If Supermom was a "product" of a broken home, she overcompensated for the lack of the other parent with her children because she definitely did not want her children to feel the real pangs and lacks of the absent parent. Whatever they wanted, she would find a way to get it for them out of guilt, shame, or proving to the world "we are not broken".

Supermom functioned in her role so well; sometimes her own children felt this was her "sole purpose for living...to do anything they asked. When she could not deliver, they would get "an attitude". Some became so blinded by her "supermom" powers they begin to see her only as a Mom, and not a woman. If they are boys growing up to be men this can cause some serious disconnect in how they related to women in their lives." They grow well into adulthood with expectations of their mothers being "Supermoms forever". Supermom was their safety net, catching them whenever they would fall down. Who caught Supermom? If they were girls growing up to be women, they either became Supermoms in training or grew in the opposite direction of not wanting to be Moms at all. They were going to have a life by any means necessary. Not seeing a healthy balance growing up between womanhood and motherhood created a multigenerational cycle of "brokenness" and disconnections.

"Supermom" does not just play her role in the home; outside of her home she is able to "transform herself into "Superwoman". Superwoman is the volunteer and/or the chaperone for all the field trips, games, the parades, events, and parties, as well as the "reliable and dedicated" employee at work. She is the community leader who because "she did not have man at home" and "didn't have anything else to do" would stay after work to finish the project. She is expected to come early, prepare for the meetings, or be the "catch all" for anything else no one else wants to do. She had convinced herself that "she had to go" because if "she didn't go" or" didn't do it" "it" would not get done. This is what she told herself "to buffer" the truth of her self value and worth. Unbeknownst to Supermom/Superwoman this obsessive role enabled many to avoid or not be responsible for doing it themselves or taking care of their own business.

If Superwoman did have a man at home, when she got there she had to "super serve him up". Some of us are old enough to remember the perfume commercial jingle, "She brings home the bacon, fry it up in the pan, and never, never, ever let him forget he's a man.....she's a Woman. (In my younger "superwoman" days, I would be proud to sing this jingle). Unbeknownst to Superwoman she sacrificed her well being just to prove to everyone she was not "broken". Eventually Superwoman will make her next "transformation" into a "machine". Objectified for what she could do, not for who SHE IS ->A WOMAN. Just like a machine, "burnt out", broke down, and obsolete. Sooner or later one of the balls will drop. The ball "Who" usually drops is "Her". Superwoman was going to perform her duties "even if even if it killed her. Isn't this why she became supermom from the beginning, not to appear "broken"?

Yes, the Supermom/Superwoman does get rewards, recognitions, pats on the backs, and a little gift now and then. But external rewards, recognitions, and pats on the backs did not give her the strength to carry on. After the award ceremony was over, she still have to go home back to her "real" life yes feeling "a little more appreciated" and but more overwhelmed and exhausted. Now, she is more stressed because these external rewards, the recognitions, and/or pats on the back often bring more expectations.

Be clear this is not an "anti man or anti single dad" expression. This is a "pro – single mom/woman, being and actualizing her true self to the fullest. This is about living life in balance and harmony inside and out. This is about showing up as who you are with wide enough space to be all you are destined to be. This is about telling the "whole truth" and nothing but "the truth" about who we are as mothers and women. So that baggage we carry can be released, liberating us to be respected, and related to from a place of wholeness.

If the truth be told, we did not do it alone. You see Superwoman's power, resilience, and strength came from an unseen yet powerful source," The Divine Power of God". Yes, God was the Father, the Mother, the Husband, the Provider, and the Protector. God was always there as her source and supplier when the purse and the cupboards were bare. The Divine Power of God got her out of bed in the morning even when she was tired and "today was not the day, and she was not the one". God was who she prayed to when she had to face those she knew did not value, appreciate, respect, and would exploit her. She was equipped with a spiritual armor made out of the greatest gifts of love, comfort, strength, and assurances that "this too shall pass". The Unconditional Love of God was her comforter when it seemed that everyone had turned their backs to her. The Divine magnet of God pulled to her Earth Angels who came to her as physical manifestations of God with love, compassion, and support at the exact time she needed it the most. It was the Divine Spirit of God that watched over and protected her children from harm when they were in and out of her protective sight. It was her Divine Wisdom that directed her to pay attention and listened with her "Divine Intuition" when to stay, when to go, when to work, when to rest, and how to be God's partner in growing, nurturing, maintaining, and sustaining life.

Superwoman is just the "outer" garment, the covering, the mask. The garment that hides our fears, our pains, our tiredness, our discomfort, and dis "ease". The cape has got to come off to enable us to come into our true selves and all of its wholeness, birthright, full humanity in order to receive our

Livin Out of Boxes...Letting Go of Bags!

Divine Inheritance. Our capes must come off for everyone we encounter in our lives to respect us and see us as our true selves. We must remove the dichotomous mask of being "super independent and don't need no help" or "super helpless not able to do nothing for ourselves". We must not accept anything less than the Divine Love God has given us. We must not enter into spaces of chaos, confusion, gossip or drama. We must enter all spaces and places in our lives bringing balance, peace, and harmony and the highest good, not bargaining with nor accepting anything less. We must be ourselves, see ourselves and express ourselves in all our gracefulness, strength, creativity, brilliance, wisdom, sensuality, sexuality, and passion. We must see ourselves as true partners and equal contributors in actualizing the Greatness of our families, communities, nations, and the world.

The covering has to come off for the women whose shoulders we stand as far back as Eve to leave a different legacy for the little girls and boys who are born seconds ago. We must believe that we are worthy of true love because we are the givers and receiver of Love. We are Love.

Single Moms are not Fragile, Not Broken, Just Tired...Superwoman has left the building!

ANGELA SIMS-WINFREY

Family and Friends, Our Lifetime Treasures

Treasure: accumulated or stored wealth in the form of money, jewels, or other valuables; one considered especially precious or valuable.

To treasure: to prize highly as valuable, rare, or costly

The families we are born into are the people that our Divine Spirits have chosen to nurture us and grow us through our Divine journeys of this lifetime. Our families are the living reflections of what we have come here to heal and overcome. Our friends are our "chosen families" magnetically drawn to us to further our maturity and growth. Think of all the blessings and lessons we have received as a result of our family struggles. These struggles pulled or push us through our "growing pains". Without them we would not have the blessings that have brought us to where we are today. Our families are the mirrors of our pleasures and pains. They mirror us so much its "uncomfortable". Our families and friends are the intimate relationships that facilitate us into a "web" of human connections from the day we are born and throughout our life. From the time we are born we are surrounded by a world full of human meanings and intentions that shape our life experiences. We live our lives in direct reflections of how we felt about ourselves as kids, how we were treated, and the ways we got disappointed. Our beliefs about ourselves are "filtered" through our interaction with our families and in relationship with our friends. These valuable relationship experiences shape the understandings of our present life. When we are facing "rough" challenges in our life that we cannot explain, we "dump" our trash on them and project our anger onto them instead of stopping to pay attention to what "treasures" they are giving us that will evolve our growth.

We think only about our "physical" growth within our families and forget that our emotional, mental, and spiritual developments are within our families. How many family members are now on someone' couch or talk shows expressing their pains that stemmed from family experiences?

"What we don't acknowledge in private the public will know. What we don't heal will spread and grow".

Through life's distorted lens and painful memories, we forget our parents, siblings, relatives, and our multitude of ancestors are products of their own life experiences with all the joys and pains that shaped their lives. It is through the lens of their knowing and experiences they raised and nurtured us. If the injuries and pains of their growing up life and living are unhealed we "unconsciously" inherit them and pass the "wounded baggage "unconsciously" to the next generation. They only gave us what they have gotten. Although we say we love them with all our heart and look to them for the most support, they are they ones that we tend to overlook, judge very harshly, and forgive the least. Forgiving ourselves, our ancestors, our families, and friends are the 1st steps to "a conscious healing". Once we move on "our conscious" journey for healthier relationships with our family and friends we must develop new covenants and agreements that are mutually supportive and respectful of each other.

Over our lifetime, we have lost many of the precious treasures of our lives, our family, friends, and colleagues. Some transitioned due to age, or long illnesses, or sudden deaths – and some we feel have gone too soon. We see them one day and although they are still in our memories and heart, they are gone from our sight forever. We forget that our physical life is not forever. Sometimes we need time, space, and distance from our families and friends to step away from the pain and heal. These are the times we need to let our family and friends know that this is our "healing time and growing space". We must also be respectful of their boundaries and "healing and growing spaces". We cannot allow our growing pains and injuries to "imprison us" and take away our power of healing and growing through our relationships with our family and friends. We cannot let unresolved conflicts and disagreements become the final chapter in our family relationships. We must be quick to love, be appreciative, be kind to each other, make the people in our lives feel special, and never let a day go by without forgiving them and forgiving ourselves. The accumulated wealth of learning and lessons from our families are invaluable. Our families share with us their rare gems of genius and pearls of wisdom whether we want to hear it or not. They are rare and precious treasures that cannot be replicated, duplicated, or imitated. There are no other relationships that are exactly like these valuable relationships. How we deal and "heal" within these relationships can be "rewarding" or costly".

> ### The Question Box
>
> *What accumulated wealth of learning we receive from our Families and Friends? What have we learned about ourselves from the wealth of learning we received from them?*

My Dear Family and Friends,

Forgive me for all the pain or injury I may have "consciously" or "unconsciously" projected to you. I forgive you for all the pain or injury or pain, "perceived or real", that you have projected unto me. My life is tied to you and my "healthy living" and freedoms are tied to me expressing my whole self in relationship with you. Whether you are with me physically, mentally, or spiritually, you are a Divine Treasure of my life, and it is my hope that I am to you. In my journey of a more conscious state of life and living, I express myself to you in a new covenant of unconditional love.

In my new relationship with you:

Livin Out of Boxes...Letting Go of Bags!

- I must stop being hurt by disagreements and respect them for what they are. They are just different points of views from different lens of experiences.

- Although we come from the same family, we are not the same; we are "unique beings who have different life learning/growing paths and purposes.

- I must be more take some time away from "doing" and" be" more present in your lives by making the most of the "precious time" we are together.

- I must be more intentional about setting boundaries in my life for my growth, as well as respectful of your personal spaces and boundaries.

- I must allow my tongue more freedom to speak from my heart, and less from my ego.

- If an agreement is broken or a conflict goes unresolved, I will do anything within my power to repair it.

- I must be more mindful and careful of my words and not let the destructive power of gossip, slander, talking behind each other's back or prejudgments roll off my tongue.

- The hurts of the past, although still in our memories have passed and there is nothing none of us can do to change it. I cannot learn from them, grow from them, heal from them, and live with them today as a dominant power. There is just not enough space. I will not give the past the power to rule my behaviors in my relationships today. My points of power exist in the present.

- My relationship with my family is more important than "the things" in my life. Things come and go. Our relationships and how we are with them last forever. Everything is of and from God to use for the greatest good.

- That as you go though your "growing pangs of life" I will touch in with you, if nothing more than to make sure you know that you are not alone and your are Love

- That as we watch the one's who came before us, the younger ones are watching us and how we relate to each and are greatly influence by what we do not what we say.

- That our children as they grow into adulthood will have some great and challenging experiences, take risk, make some choices that may set them back, or propel them forward just as our experience and choices have done for us.

- Our children will be okay, "God got them", just as he had us when we made our choices and decisions.

- *I know I must respond to all my abilities to raise and nurture those who are entrusted in my care and let them go to fly with their own wings.*

- *I must release my "perceived control" over your life and avoid tools of manipulation such as guilt and humiliation to get my way. I should just know that it the midst of "my" frustration, I need to just go sit somewhere and relax. God is in Control!*

- *I must release my feeling that if you are not doing it like I do it or have done like I did it; nothing is getting done or will get done.*

- *I must get out of your way and stay in the lane of my Divine path and purpose.*

- *I now know for sure that I am because you are and have been in my life a Divine expression of God's Greatness and you will be treasure in my life and heart forever.*

I will spend my time, energy, and attention being more intentional about expressing my love for you being the Divine Treasures of my life.

ANGELA SIMS-WINFREY

Actualize.....

Faith

Treasure...

Family

Appreciate...

Friends!

Livin Out of Boxes...Letting Go of Bags!

Healing Path Three...Unpacking Boxes and Bags

ANGELA SIMS-WINFREY

Livin' Out of Boxes...

Institution: An organization, establishment, foundation, society or the like devoted to a particular cause or program. **Institutionalized:** to accustom (a person) so firmly to the care or supervised routine of an institution as to make incapable of managing life outside of it.

Livelihood: a means of supporting one's existences financially or vocationally; your "bread and butter. **Lively:** full of life and energy; vibrant.

Many of us who work institutionally or influenced by societal norms do our works" for someone in exchange for compensation, in service, or to build our resume "up the ladder to success". We train for, prepare for, and "dress for success" to be interviewed for the world of work that will surely provide for a lifetime of fulfillment, esteem, and financial stability. In our institutional and societal work, when we do our jobs well and are rewarded through payments, awards, and recognitions; our value and worth increases tremendously. Some of us have been "so programmed" to meet or exceed the institutional and/or societal demands and expectations of us, we forget that we "brought" anything to the table. Many of us as people of color are so "socialized" to run "twice as fast or jump "twice" as high to get "half as much", we walk in the door "devaluing" ourselves and anyone who looks like us. We have become "institutionalized" to the point that we do not know who we are without a "relationship" to an institution. Some of our identities are so tied to institutions we will "sacrifice our families or lay down our lives (stressfully and literally) for it.

The messages of lack and limitations are so pervasive, when the institutions we work for are "hurting" we "start hurting". Some of us begin to believe that we and the institution are one

and the same. We have really been lead to believe the "man-made up hype", that if we keep working hard for the "plantation", it will take care of us and our families. Some of us may not be on the plantation, but we are functioning as "indentured servants, enslaved or sharecropping". At the end of our "servitude" we have very little to show for our "hard works". This speaks "volumes" as to how and where we put our time, energy, and attention, and for what purpose. Many of our ancestors were forced to work under these circumstances, but through faith, resilience, they persevered through pain, shame, (mentally and physically) and humiliation (more than we could ever imagine) not just for their personal freedom, but for future generations to "be free".

Our belief and devotion to the institutions we work as "our source and supply" has gotten us "trapped under the "illusion of security" and the box of perceived success. There are some who just "stay neutral" for fear that if we are "silent" or invisible enough the dark shadow of the "institutional head cutter" will overlook us. If we miss the first "round of cuts", we believed that we have been spared for the moment. Either way this type of environment manifests an atmosphere of anxiety and fear. In this mode, the people around us start exhibiting some "not so strange" behaviors. We now notice that some or our colleagues or co-workers seem to be more distant. They do not want to be seen no where near you, less known have you to close to them to "bring your dimming light" by them. Some of our "fearful co-workers" begin to do whatever it takes, by any means necessary, even to slander you or lie about you to prove that they are more valuable than you or "keep their spot". There are games of "divide and conquer". Some call it a "dogs eat dog" world. Dogs don't eat other dogs". Dogs are trained to fight other dogs or if neglected and abuse attack for "survival". If a dog is loved, cares for, and nurtured, it is a lifelong, devoted companion.

Anyway we are not dogs, are any other animals, and we should stop excusing our behaviors by acting out and not taking responsibility for our behaviors and actions toward ourselves and others. Even when the institution or organization's foundation (integrity) has been "cracked", and fail to live by it's "founding" principles and values, some of us still are at the "stage of bargaining" with our own integrity to stay attached to its insecurity. We hang around looking for the next "institutional hit or event" to give us some "signs" of getting back to how it use to be. When "the cracks" of an "unhealed foundation" are allowed to spread, sooner or later the entire structure will come tumbling down and we will be one of its "broken up" casualties.

There is not one institution established by man that was set up for everyone to thrive. Institutions are set up to only to use "pieces" of the work we offer and throw away the other" pieces or people" that does not feed it. The "majority" of the man-made institutions were set up to benefit whom they always benefit by maintaining the status quo. The "same quo" that has been "status" and empowered by the authority of the state has become the 1% that holds the majority of the wealth of nation. This 1% and its "political puppets" that benefit would rather die with this wealth in their graves before they share it with anyone who does not "play in their backyard". When "the political puppets" feel their benefactors are being threaten, the self-preservation mode button is automatically turned on and will "by any means necessary" protect their institutions at all cost. Even at the cost of "their souls" or lives of the people who work there. Most governmental social service agencies, non-profit "501 © 3" agencies and organizations they sanctioned are set up as social control mechanism" for both the "nonprofit and those it serves". In the midst of being held hostage in this economic monopoly, the temporary relief or support we need "rolls" into a prolonged cycle of dependency. This eventually contributes to a multigenerational process of disempowerment and economic disenfranchisement.

Livin Out of Boxes...Letting Go of Bags!

These institutional boxes are so fill up with "dehumanizing boxes and bags" they are imploding. The only way we are able to either mentally, physically, or spiritually get out and stay out of these oppressive spaces is to "empty" our bags of these rotten messages discard them in disintegrators, or dumpsters where they belong.

Now I know some of what I just shared may be difficult for some to digest. As I am healing this myself, my throat gets a little tight. If this does not apply to you and you "got it going on", just keep "doing" what you are "doing". I am on a pathway of healing my "doing" in balance with "being". The digestion of these messages become easier as I open myself up to the broader view of the spaces and places that I am doing my Divine Work. Sometimes the truth hurts and its hard to digest.

Be clear, I am not saying that we should not do our "divine works and share our talents, skills, and spiritual gifts" inside institutions. Fear, lack, insecurity does not align with God's Divine Purpose for our Life, Living, and Livelihood. What I am speaking to is our state of mind and purpose of our work intentions and motivations while we are in there. What I am saying is that we have to know where we are sharing our "spiritual gifts and divine works". There is an "ole school" country song that says you gotta know when to hold em...know when to fold em... know when to walk away...and know when to run...

"Do not give dogs what is sacred; do not throw your pearls to pigs. If you do, they may trample them under their feet, and then turn and tear you to pieces. Matt 7:6

In this present day and time some of us have no other choice of where we work. However, we must make sure that the time, energy and attention that we are investing in our work are providing the support for our family and community's sustenance and well-being.

We must keep the belief that God is our Source and Supplier. We don't have to sell our souls or "bargain-basement" our compensations, rewards, or blessings in "this God's Kingdom of Abundance and Prosperity".

The Question Box

Are we working for the servitude of the "institution" or for the "common good" of our families and our communities"? Is our work our "livelihood" or a place that we are just "serving time"?

Livin Out of Boxes...Letting Go of Bags!

Job Title and Job Decriptions

Divine Work or Distractions?

In all my work life I use my Spiritual Gifts as a leader, messenger, an organizer and facilitator to improve the conditions of people "cast aside" by society. Whether it was to address poverty, housing, health and healthcare, or social justice and equity this work was always my passion. I always felt that the work I did was an assignment from God. Did this make me a messenger of God? How can this be possible? Aren't messengers of God angels? Aren't angels' spiritual beings that have specific assignments from God by protecting, guarding and bringing the truths "big truths" to specific people who find themselves in critical situations? If we are moving to a "New Earth" how are people moved to this new "space and place"? As I was moved by God to grow a more in depth spiritual understanding and strengthen my "inner knowing", this role became clearer. How do I know that this role was "anointed" by God? These roles and work functions have been my name, my spiritual gifts, values, passion and principles of how I worked were a reflection of these roles. The job titles, job positions, the job descriptions and places I perform these gifts were only where I was "positioned" for that moment to strengthen my spiritual gifts and grow my Divine talents for a greater purpose.

I feel in the depth of my soul that this is the role of my Divine Purpose. When I perform this work in places and environments that ignited these functions, and nurtured my growth, I excitedly and passionately perform the task at hand. When I felt I had "outgrown" or was being smothered, diminished, not respected, or unappreciated, wherever my ego was attached would determine if I would "stay to long" or move on. However, whether you know what your purpose is or not in order to grow you will have lessons and test. Once you learned your lessons and past the test, you will grow and evolve in your Divine Purpose. If your ego gets in the way, it stagnate your growth, and you will encounter the same challenges in your next workplace and location.

Growing my spiritual gifts of discernment and sharing the messages I received were my "biggest" challenge. To be able listen with my heart and share messages of truths that "relatable", respected, and received by the people drawn into the spaces and places my experiences led me was very difficult when my "insecure" ego was "amped up". In my journey of affirming my role and purposes I had to be tested by "external noises" that were the measurements of my growth about whether I was "listening". When I absorb these "noises" mostly given out of frustration and attempts to control, it was in conflict with my soul messages that "resisted" the noises. I was wondering how they could know I was not listening. For them to know this they had to be "inside my ear". The more they said I didn't listen the more frustrated I became and the more frustrated they became. Ego was shouting at ego, and both were seeking to defend and protect itself. When messages are pass through an ego filter it manifest emotional frustrations. The ego becomes more dominant than what is being shared. When I was told I wasn't listening, my ego "jumped" into defense mode and all I heard was "criticism". My spiritual gift of discernment knew whether it was "constructive, unconstructive or destructive. However, I did not know how to express my discomfort with what was being said. My lack of confidence in expressing myself when challenged short-circuited my communication which further exasperated an environment of frustration. When my ego felt attacked, my "ear listening" shut down, and I went into "mute mode", to protect my "heart".

You see at this time my" insecure ego" and my identity were tied more to the organizational expectations or "societal norms" than to my Divine Works. I allowed the organization or "my colleagues" going through life challenges like myself define me and distract me away from my Divine Purpose.

The more I developed and grew my "inner listening"; I was able to become less of a "victim" of my ego and more of a "monitoring witness" to it. This help me to understand when to put my ego is "in check" in balance with my "whole being". To become an evolved messenger, I had to develop my "inner listening" and detach my message from my ego. I had to check my "perceptions" and "prejudgments" to be able to receive and absorb the messages and lessons I needed for my growth and my journey in maturing into a Divine Messenger.

As a "new spiritual reality" is evolving I truly believe that there are multigenerational "Divine Messengers of God" being prepared to deliver and facilitate "healthy" (healing} transitions and transformation for people to be present in this "new space and place". Whether the title is Earth Angels, Divine Messengers, Teachers, Facilitators, Evangelist, or Ministers, it should be representative of Divine Work as an expression of God not "our ego". Societal titles attached to egos are conditional and temporary. Divine Work last a lifetime. Divine Work that serve and benefit "the common good" sustains itself for generations. For us to become effective in actualizing our Divine Work, we must know what our Spiritual Gifts are, grow and evolve them into talents and skills to share. We must pay attention to who, why, where, when, and how we share these gifts for growth, development, and fostering divine centered empowerment in communion (common union) with others. When we share our Divine works for the common good, our rewards and blessings will be there for us to take care of our responsibilities and receive the desires of our heart. When we focus more on our job titles, our job status, or institutional positions, it diminishes our Divine Authority to serve people. What's important is how we express our Divine Work.

ANGELA SIMS-WINFREY

Sistahs Betsy, Camille, Irene, and Katrina

Women Scorned or Calls to Wisdom?

Women and children were the bore the heaviest burden and were the most "impacted victims" in the aftermaths of the Gulf Coast Disaster". Women's ways of life as mothers, wives, workers, head of majority of the households, and caretakers has been shattered and deteriorated in the aftermaths of this disaster. Women of color disproportionately victimized by arbitrary displacement, lack of quality education, lack of affordable housing, job discrimination, and denial of voting rights, inadequate health and transportation. In the hurricane's aftermaths and recovery efforts, women have also been have also been victimized by increased violence, mental, and physical abuse. Women from the Gulf Coast representing thousands of women from "back of town", "across the tracks", across the canal, "the hood", the projects, with "peculiar" linkages up with women from the suburbs, and uptown raised their voices in the streets. They cried out their "pressure cooked" frustration of the blatant indifference and neglect from "irresponsible and unaccountable" local, state and national officials. They aired their disdained for "deaf eared" dismissal of the multigenerational words of warning and wisdom", that we need to "get ready" for the Big One.

Many have used the word "strength" to describe African American and indigenous women's way of life. This strength is wrapped up in a spirit of nurturing, tolerance and resilience in which women have overcame many of life's adversities. These strengths were stretched beyond human capacity when once again these man-made systems proved again indifference toward women and their families. On all levels of these "hierchial structures" failed. They failed to provide adequate evacuation plans, assistance, and humanitarian aid constituted grave violations of basic human rights. As Hurricane Katrina

Livin Out of Boxes...Letting Go of Bags!

ripped pass the Gulf Coast on August 29th, the blown away covers exposed the multigenerational faces of disempowerment. The faces of mostly African American women, splatters of indigenous and poor whites praying over their children and lost love ones paralyzed many in front of television screens across the nation and around the world. It was not hard to feel and see the pain, shock and helplessness of many women who just a day earlier was the picture of strength, hope, and determination.

Several days before Hurricane Katrina, most families fled through a "hodge podge" of evacuation avenues. Those who remain were mostly elderly, disabled, and African American women, women of color, poor women and their children who disproportionately lacked personal transportation. This was known well in advance of Hurricane Katrina. Public transportation was only used as a last resort for those remaining in the city to bring to the Superdome. Most city buses and school buses were left to drown in parking lots.

"Untold stories" that will reflect the many women and children who were left in neighborhoods and shelters of last resort to be exposed and/or victimized over and over again.

"Untold stories" released the multigenerational bags stored of hurricanes that many women have held since Hurricane Betsy in 1965. Forty years of devaluing and dehumanizing messages of denial, tolerance, classism, colorism manifested by racism fostered a multigenerational, perpetuating process of "surplus disempowerment. Internalized message of worthlessness evidenced by memories of Hurricane Betsy when the city officials made the decision to open the levee on "the black side", the Lower 9th Ward so that floodwaters would not get to the "white side" of the city. These multigenerational memories re-triggered by similarities of which areas of Hurricane Katrina got flooded the most. This time the messages were evidenced by those on "higher ground" and those on "lower ground". An historical "set up" based on a "race construct" of where some people choose to live and where others "had to live". These "recycled" messages created an ongoing sense of insecurities and anxieties. Throughout these years the way of life for these women was to stay "prayed up" and prepare to keep their families whole and safe from the next "big one". "Livin' out of boxes and water-proof containers was a "hurricane season" ritual as many families put special items in the attics and go to "higher ground" whenever a hurricane came into the Gulf of Mexico. Due to the "breached" and overtopped levees, in the aftermaths of Katrina, many women and their families became the "special things" forced into attics, in trees, and on rooftops to avoid death from the rising waters.

In the aftermaths of Hurricane Katrina, the poorest of the poor before the hurricane, socially marginalized women of color will be the last to leave the social controlled, "toxic" trailer encampments and dilapidated apartments assigned by FEMA. These women were mostly elderly women, public housing residents, residents of mobile homes, and renter-often women headed households being the sole source of income. Most of the public housing development, the strongest and safer structures, remained barricaded with steeled doors and fenced off. Permanent housing for these women and their families with more permanency is still not a priority. Many remain displaced without adequate support mechanisms due to family and social support networks being ripped away by the aftermaths of the storm.

Hurricane Katrina's aftermaths and fragmented recovery efforts rendered everything out of control and exasperated "unhealed" post-traumatic stress disorders. This has taken its toll on the strongest women. The instability and uncertainties of life stresses and has caused implosions of mental, physical and spiritual health. The lack of primary health care, and mental health care and long waits in emergency room have worsened and equally have made it impossible to control chronic diseases. This lack of health care and "stress-related" "dis"

Livin Out of Boxes...Letting Go of Bags!

eases caused a dramatic surge of "untimely" deaths and even now if you read the obituary most are women. Many "internally displaced" women and their families whose family homes were washed away or demolished are still seeking "welcoming" spaces and places to "re-root" and "re-home" their lives.

Hurricanes Betsy, Camille, Katrina, and Irene were painful manifestations of women who have been marginalized, violated, disrespected, rejected, and neglected. Are these the expressions of women scorned or is this another "distorted " sound bite that attempts to diminish the pains of women's trials and tribulations to just being "angry black women". These women name Hurricane's were often connected to "sayings" such as "hell has no fury like a women scorn". This "saying is often misquoted, partially used from a quote of a literary play entitled, The Mourning Bride which says "Heaven as no rage like love to neither hatred turn, nor hell has a fury like a woman scorned". Shouldn't these women be angered and scorned? Of coursed! When you are impacted by a "never-ending" story of disrespect, neglect, mental, physical, and environment abuse you begin to feel angry, numbed or disconnected from your own humanity. Anger sometimes become the only release in blowing the top off the "pressure cooker" .

The rhetoric around just stereotyping "black women" as angry and scorn belittles the real and underlying "unhealed wound" of constantly be relegated to the lowest rung of "racially constructed" ladder. The anger comes from these internalized messages constantly being "trigger" by a perpetual cycle of the "same ole stuff" oppressing and neglecting them over and over again.

ANGELA SIMS-WINFREY

The strength and resilience of the "black woman" is evidence of her ability to "keep her family together", holding together the pieces of moral integrity for restoration and reclamation of human dignity in the midst of recovery.

Let us never forget that...

...A Woman is an expression of God Divine Love and Wisdom!

Wisdom calls aloud in the street, she raises her voice in the public squares; at the head of the noisy streets she cries out, in the gateways of the city she makes her speech:

How long will you simple ones love your simple ways? How long will mockers delight in mockery and fools hate knowledge? If you had responded to my rebuke, I would have poured out my heart to you and made my thoughts known to you. And as we all know, hell hath no fury like a woman scorned.

But since you rejected me when I called and no one gave heed when I stretched out my hand. Since you ignored all my advice and would not accept my rebuke, I in turn will laugh at your disaster;

I will mock when calamity overtakes you — when calamity overtakes you like a storm, when disaster sweeps over you like a whirlwind, when distress and trouble overwhelm you.

Livin Out of Boxes...Letting Go of Bags!

Then they will call to me but I will not answer; they will look for me but will not find me. Since they hated knowledge and did not choose to fear the Lord, since they would not accept my advice and spurned my rebuke, they will eat the fruit of their ways and be filled with the fruit of their schemes.

For the waywardness of the simple will kill them, and the complacency of fools will destroy them; But those who listen to me will be secure and will live at ease, without fear of harm and dread of disaster ...Proverbs 1:20-33

Only fools make fun of what they can't overshadow, what cannot be explained gets blamed, what makes us uncomfortable gets ridicule and shame. We must disconnect and "detox" our spirits from the "negative socialized connotations women. We should embrace that what motherly-natured, Sistahs Betsy, Camille, and Katrina were actually expressing their ...

ANGELA SIMS-WINFREY

Sticks and Stones!

Bag Lady, Welfare Queen, Drug Addict, Crack Baby, Deadbeat….

Low Life… Ghetto…Illegal Alien….Hillbilly…P.W. T.

The Bags of ignorant sticks and stones you hurl at me.

Evacuee, Refugee, Homeless, or Internally Displaced

All the names you call me not to see my face.

Labels, tags, markings, that distance me from you

Is it because you are fear, seeing me reflects all you don't or do?

Giving me labels or tags will not make me go away.

I am lurking in the shadows of your background waiting for the day.

To open your eyes, your heart, your soul,

To face the realities of life so big, so bold.

Living out loud, speaking so proud

Removing the shroud you have placed over me.

All up in your face, taking my place;

Fulfilling a destiny in store for me.

To be free to fulfill a Divine Holy will,

Livin Out of Boxes...Letting Go of Bags!

Purposely living, giving, sharing, caring,

Guiding, gliding, bearing gifts of

Truth, Hope, and Love;

Gifts given at birth from Heaven above.

So keep using your labels to run from the truth

You can run but you can't hide, they are coming after you.

Because the seeds you spit from your mouth is reaping what you will sow

What you plant in my garden, in yours will grow.

So be careful the names of God's children you call

Keep checking behind you, your words will stumble your fall.

Throw your sticks and stones,

They may hurt my heart and break my bones,

Pay attention to your words.

They "come back" and expose your reality!

ANGELA SIMS-WINFREY

Lettin' Go of Bags!

Living in these man-made, "ego-driven" institutional boxes has distracted so many of us away from our Divine Purpose. In the race to meet our institutional obligations, our spiritual obligations have fallen by the wayside. When we are not consistent in growing, nurturing, and gratefully appreciative of our Spiritual Gifts, we become reactive victims to "man constructed" institutions. The protectors of institutional stability "evaluate us, which mean they determine our worth and value by their standards and through their limited view of our actions. We take it as personal hits to who we are. We begin to "internalized" these dehumanizing messages of our "stock being devalued, going down or worst - crashing. We get fed "dehumanizing" and "disempowering" messages daily. When we do "get a shock" of reality, we panic and all the "fear factors" of our self-survival mode get's activated. Our hopes, dreams, and security get's "deactivated". We move ourselves into a "voluntary prison of disconnect and isolation. In this prison our ego plays all day and night with the "yo yo" of lack and limitations. It is having such a "good" time; it draws our "like minded" play cousins – "Cousin Fear" and "Cousin Doubt" unto the "playground". The next thing we know our "Cousin Shame and Guilt" have skipped in. When "Cousin Anger and Cousin Rage" races in "all hell breaks" loose, now "Big Cousin Self-Destruction" is on the way. Before you know it we have surrendered control to anything or anyone that shows up to the "open invitation" that started out as a "Whoa is Me Pity Party". Boundaries no longer exist between "what's real" and "what's Memorex". We begin existing in a perpetual cycle of "victimhood".

There are those who on the other end drawn to the "magnified" space with" over inflated" egos, who denial of the changes of their circumstances. They are so distorted; they walk into the space with the belief that they are entitled to whatever remains in the space. They pretend they are okay and "suck" everything out of the space for themselves. Some of us keep functioning in denial on "auto pilot" as if this job or institutional work condition will come back. Some of us are so "dis eased" with discomfort; we do whatever it takes to "bargain" our way back to our "not so comfort zones". Our natural born Spiritual Gifts, the talents, and the skills we learned and earned are all but forgotten because we sold it "so cheaply" to the institution. Our lives are more valuable than what we do and what we have.

Another manifestation of "victimhood" is to deny any responsibility we have had in creating the circumstances we now find ourselves in. We blame anyone we can to avoid feeling "flawed" by our mistakes, unconscious, or lower conscious decisions and actions. If we can't explain, we blame it on our "primal instincts", weaken state of mind, or our addictive behaviors,

Some of our response to our "flawed actions", rude, or disrespectful behavior is "the devil made me do it" or "the devil is busy". 1st and foremost, "the devil cannot do anything or walk into our thoughts and behaviors unless our "weaken" spirit" or "dis – eased egos" invite it in. 2nd, all biblical readings or scriptures that I have read or absorbed describes "the devil, satan, or evil" as a tempter who lies or use false trickeries to lure, entice, seduce, distract, or persuade people or persons from their Divine Purpose. If you are grounded in your faith and clear on your purpose, "no one" or "no thing" can distract you. When did "the devil" become more powerful than God? Even in all the temptations of Christ, the devil did not have the power to make him do anything against "his free will", and his strong reverence to God. The devil is a minor distraction that only is relevant if we give whatever/whomever he/or it suppose to be relevance. We may get tempted, however, we have been blessed with free will, and choice to act on the temptation or not.

In "the pressures of survival", we become "arm chair" quarterbacks in judging and critiquing other people's lives. What we witness as "we peek" in the lives of others, is a very small fraction of the "totality of their life experiences". It is our own fearful and "clouded lens" that we are peeping out of and projected unto others. When we are bunkered down" in a survival mode, our fearful ego blinds us to our own behaviors and actions. Life seems so surreal. One day our life "appears" to be going well, and the next day, it has been altered by some "seen" and "unseen" forces. Our worry and fears make us act out or "shut down" in ways that are confusing to us. We just don't understand. Nothing we seem to do is right. Any glimmer of hope is temporary and appears to fade as soon as you get it. Everything around you starts to break down. We begin to feel so broken, so judged, isolated, so alone, so insecure…….

STOP! IN THE NAME OF GOD'S UNCONDITIONAL LOVE!

WHAT OUR "INSECURE" EGO IS TELLING US IS A BIG LIE. WHAT WE ARE FEELING IS JUST A TEMPORARY ILLUSION. THE SPIRITUAL GIFTS WE HAVE GOTTEN IS OUR BIRTHRIGHT. THE TALENTS AND SKILLS WE HAVE ABSORBED AND GAIN ARE NOT LOST, THEY NEVER LEFT, OUR SPIRITUAL GIFTS ARE STILL HERE. WE JUST HAVE TO TAP INTO GOD'S DIVINE POWER USE THEM.

TRUE SECURITY COMES FROM GOD…BREATHE…

Livin Out of Boxes...Letting Go of Bags!

"Broken Wings"

Broken...adj: fragmented, torn, not functioning properly, not in working order......**verb**: smashed, divided, ignored, violated, wounded, injured, humiliated, reduced, rejected

Wings...noun: movable organ for flying, an arm of a human, in flight, under one's protection; **verb:** do something without fear, doubt, act without over thinking, move on spiritual or intuition, to take risk, a means, a way....freedom.

The Question Box

What is going on? Why am I not moving beyond this condition? How did I get here? Where are my angels of deliverance?

The truth and nothing but the truth, is an oath taken when a witness or defendant takes "the stand", to share what they have done or witness. When we come to "our growing stumbles" of life...our life's test, we take the stand in reflected inquiries of the whys, what's, who's, and where's of our actions or views that got us to the circumstances (full circles) of our conditions of today. When we take these stands we indict ourselves, put ourselves on trial, judge ourselves, convict ourselves, and sentence ourselves before anyone else enters the equations. The first automatic indictments are our "egoic" reactions to fears of brokenness. In order to protect itself, when our ego feels threaten expressed by our emotions of defensiveness or anger, we blame anything or everyone around us for these conditions. This automatic reaction is a natural deflection of shielding ourselves or the world away from our "perceived" brokenness or imperfections. One minute we are moving, going, living and the next minute we feel scattered, fragmented, torn, and stagnated to the point of malfunction then put aside for not being in working order.

"ANTs". (Automatic Negative Thoughts) are driven by an underlying devaluing of ourselves for what we do as oppose to the core of who we are. If we move away from our thoughts and go deeper to hear our inner spiritual voice we will know that this is a signal to move into learning new lessons for spiritual growth. If we stay with the "ANTS" and feed them by connecting with other "ANTS" we stall our growth, and open ourselves to "external noises", and prolong our state of pain and insecurities. "Like draws like". These outside distractions leave our spiritual wounds unattended and more divided, ignored, injured, humiliated, reduced, and rejected leaving us in vicious cycle of paralysis or stuck somewhere complaining about the same challenges and people over and over again. While we are in pain, we go from person to person sharing our pain, seeking answers, but unbeknownst us, our ego's in this state is only seeking validation to keep the pain alive. We keep looking and searching for something outside of ourselves for the answers. We ask anyone we encounter for answers forgetting that if our spirits are low and egos are "closed off" in fear and doubt, we will attract those who are fearful and doubtful.

In order to not open "the floodgate" of the playground of despair, we must stop sitting in the judge's chair or jury box with all our "playground friends", hurling self imposed judgments on ourselves and everyone else when our fears are magnified. We must stop "playing God" in our "egoic" perceptions of power and control that gets manifested by manipulation and "tricks". "Tricks and game playing" are for kids and if we play too long, we will get trapped on that playground. Once we actualize our "free will" and keep God in the center of our decision making, our spiritual healing and strengthening will begin. The people, spaces, and places of those who are still in "the playground" will be revealed. Our "broken wings" will be held together and healed.

In my spiritual journey of healing, I was constantly wondering and seeking answers for why I was experiences so much pain in my life from "perceived loss". I was searching in my own life reflections all the little needles in the "haystack" of my life choices, decisions, and experiences that could be the indictments of my sins and failures. Because I have always had a belief in the power of God, I begin to judge myself for "wavering in faith, and being impatient. There were periods of time in my darken state of doubt and fear that I felt my faith wavering. I then started feeling guilty for having these thoughts.

I sentence myself to a barrage of negative thoughts and self imposed isolation, only coming out to perform my "doing" duties". Sometimes the collection of negative dust from past memories would collect in my thoughts and weigh me down so powerfully. All of a sudden the beliefs I held on to so strongly would appear to be sinking. Fostering a feeling that the circumstances or the condition I was in today was going to be a life sentence. I started believing that it was my duty and destiny to be a facilitator of others happiness and joy and the sooner I accept this "ego-fed" fact, the better I would feel.

In my midst of this struggle and shifting, I remained faithful and little sparkles of hope would push it way through my soul opening up new spiritual learning and teachings. The more I learn from and practice listening to my "soul voice", the more I became a witness to the triggers of my ego-driven emotions, the less fearful I became. I was no longer a victim to my emotions; I begin to take back my power and charge of my life. I could now see beyond the pain, pay more attention, and begin counting all of my life blessings and moments of peaceful, happy, and joys. I started focusing on those beautiful little angels that were being born and coming into this earth ready to make us smile. Those little girls that my daughter drew into her life from her light of joy and hope gave me joy. Those Earth Angels that have always been there with acts of kindness, little scriptures of Divine Wisdom, and prayers are God sent blessings. I am now paying attention to the calm and peaceful people that I experienced who always seem to have a warm heart, and those who positively see the best of humanity. I avoided or quickly move myself away from those who seem to be always complaining, stereotyping and labeling those who seemed to be different or doing something different. My life's lesson has shown me that sooner or later their complaints, typecast, and judgments will turn toward me. Earth Angels are those people who come into your life at just the "right" time to share their Spiritual Gifts, talents, blessings, a prayer, a motivating affirmation, a lighthearted joke or just a loving hug. They share without judgment or conditions and see your circumstance for what it is - a temporary stumble.

They look past the surface view and see the wholeness of your humanity, not just the exposed pieces of pain that are healing and growing.

As I begin to pull back my ego, and acknowledge in my being, my actions, and my expressions God's Divine Power, my judgments of myself were starting to reduce from "perceived brokenness" to powerful reflections of my total life experiences. My egoic power was diminishing and I am no longer looking for the "negative needles" in the haystacks, I am now looking forward to the Divine Gems in the "treasure chest" of life. Those little negative needles of the past are still a "little prickly", but they no longer feel like a "thorns" in my side, back, and heart. They are being replaced by something wonderful and new. It is not just the new people and places that came or are coming into my life, there is a "new knowing" that every person, place or thing that I experienced was a necessary growing and learning experience for me to be bless to be all I am today, and all I am becoming. I now have a new vision with an evolved divine prescription of senses beyond what I can see, touch, hear, feel, or smell. I now am "growing an inner knowing" of a presence that is so much more powerful than my basic senses. This Divine Power sees and controls everything beyond anything or anyone we can see. This Divine Power knows exactly who, what, where, and when blessings are ready to be received to express a Greater Good.

When my Divine Spirit isawaken and open to new experiences my ego is no longer "in full" control of my reactions to life. I know this because as I am feeling the Divine Spirit within getting stronger and I am more aggressively fighting off the darts of doubt. I now am less afraid to push through the pain or face my fears because I know that I am not facing them alone. I know that the "egoic" enemy within and outside will pull every trick in and out of the book to penetrate my Divine Faith. Even going through those I love to be carriers of its "dis" eased egoic deeds. This is when the battle gets really hard, because now I have to strengthen my spiritual armor of "unconditional love", to love them through my injuries and pain while at the same time loving them through theirs. As the battle gets harder, I now know that I can no longer just rely on "man-made and created, duplicated, replicated, and imitated fruits to feed my mind, body and soul. All of my Divine talents, skills, and experiences under girded by my Spiritual Gifts. This will facilitate my creativity and Divine Work. The fruit I produce will multiply my blessings abundantly. In my "rejuvenated and renewed" understanding, I know for sure that God was, is, and will always be my source and supplier. I now understand "the things" I used to have, are not a loss, but have cleared a space for "something" better. In the meantime, as I wait patiently for the new blessings that God have in store for me, my family and I am being fed with God's daily bread, and nurtured by Divine food for the heart, thought, and spirit. When I go to bed every night, my basic needs of food, water, and shelter are being divinely provided. I also know from this "life changing" humbling experience, that everything is a blessing that comes from this Divine power source of abundance no matter how small it may seem. I also know that if someone has a greater need and I had the power to share it, or know where they can get relief, it is my Divine duty to share no matter what external voices or my fearful ego says. It is my responsibility to give and share with a full view of my life's blessings and let my Divine Gift of Discernment and Compassion be my spiritual guide of giving and sharing.

When someone has been given much, much will be required in return; and when someone has been entrusted with much, even more will be required... Luke 12:48

Once I am fully aware and tap into my Divine Power source, my ego cannot get me to react fearfully to my growing surroundings. My fearful egos no longer have the ability to "rush" me into other people's "not so reality shows", to please them or prove my self to them. I now know that I only have to prove myself to God. I am becoming fully conscious of the Divine Power of God. I now know I have a choice to "be stuck" in a cycle of despair or make a decision to stay plugged into God's Divine Power Source. As a human being I will be tempted to go back to the "playground" of not enough "playing with jealousy, envy, competitiveness, stinginess, hoarding, self absorption, and insecurity.

You see it is not just our ancestral or transition spiritual angels that are present in our lives; our Divine Spirits are the constant energy of our life source. It is our breath of life, it is our truth, and it is our Angel Wings given to us to soar. Our wings are not just the physical organs attached to our bodies called arms that give us the power to do things or move things in our surrounding. They are not just physical wings seen in birds, insects, and beast of flight. They are the Divine Spirit of hope, trust, and truth, powered by God's "unconditional love". Our "broken wings" can be healed. No one outside of us has the "super glue" to put our wings back together. It is not a complicated procedure. We are only required to go within ourselves for the "divine healing kit". Yes even when our human arms or limbs or broken, or a bird's wings are broken someone can assist us in holding the brokenness in place. Yes, Earth Angels do come into our lives to assist us with the wrap, the stint, the stitches, and or the tape of kindness, compassion, and love while our spiritual wing is healing and growing stronger. Our Divine Spirit is "regenerative" as the living tissues of our bodies and when we relax, and trust that God is fully in control, we surrender to a new life of Divine living. The difference between our "regenerative spirit" and our "physical regeneration" is that the physical body and things are only temporary, but our Divine Spirit lives forever.

And through the midst of it all our brokenness and pain, God is always with us and has "unconditional love" even for "Earth Angels"

With...

"Broken Wings"

ANGELA SIMS-WINFREY

Healing Path Four...Divine Liberation

Independence?

Doing it alone, is not being a leader

Doing it yourself is not helping others

Doing it how you like is not teaching someone

Doing these things are not independence

It's self hearted.

—Malaikia Sims-Winfrey

ANGELA SIMS-WINFREY

Divine Liberation
The Truth Will Set You Free!

Independent - free from external control and constraint; free - able to act at will; not hampered; not under compulsion or restraint; not united or joint; self-governed; self-sufficient.
Independence - The state or quality of being independent

Liberate - To set free, as from oppression, confinement, or foreign control. **Liberation:** the act of being liberated

Freedom - The condition of being free of restraints; liberty of the person from slavery, detention, or oppression.

On July 4th many of us celebrate our independence and freedom. Some of us will be in reflection or enjoying a day of eating, drinking, resting, and celebrating in the sun with those we love, the little ones we hug so dear, those family treasures that are near, or those who in our thoughts or in the depths of our hearts afar; Some of us will be savoring" for a moment", a temporary release from the "prisons" created from the " trappings of life.

..................Judgments, stereotypes, non-supportive, criticism discrimination, racism, self-hate, unworthiness, consumerism , addictions, financial bondage, illness, homelessness, unemployment, under employment, overworked, "dis" abilities and "the traps" of success "mentally, physically, and spiritually.

While some us see no reason to celebrate at all. Some of us are seeking a "spiritual release" from the bondage of a "tired", "dis" stressed or "dis" eases of mind and body seek to "bind" our powerful Spirit of Divine Living!

Our "inability to be truly free, independent, or liberated is due to the state or stagnation of an "egoic" mind. True freedom, as our ancestors modeled is the "ability" to surrender and release to the flow in the rhythm of the Divine Power within ourselves and in harmony with the who's, what's and "why's around" us. Are these messages "real or memorex – the multigenerational societal tapes played "over and over" defining who you are, how you should live, what you should do, and who you should do it with. Independence is not the same as freedom and liberation. Knowing, being and living "your truth" will set you free.

It was the power of Divine Faith, Wisdom, and Trust that move our ancestors to move into the action from "man made and societal bondage. It is not a "calendar" day, week, month or year. It is not "measured "in, on, of, under, or around time.

It flows in each in every one of us because ...

We Breathe............

It's a Divine Gift given to us as a "birthright" by the Highest Power that "Be". The power of God's Love gives us the freedom to be truthful, to trust, and to love without judgment or without condition.

- We have "free will".
- We have the freedom of compassion to give and share.

- We have the freedom to pray and meditate on our heart's desires.
- We have the freedom to be released from these "trappings" and be abundantly prosperous and transcend our abilities.

We have the freedom to praise, be grateful, be thankful for all of the blessings and life lessons that have flowed and will continue to flow ...due to our Divine Inheritance of Love and Life.

"Every day, every hour, every minute, every second ...

We Breathe..........

> ### The Question Box
>
> What are your truths? Are you freely being your true self or living your true life? How are you expressing your truths and true self? Are your truths covered by "perceptions" or realities? Are your truths based on messages of lack, limitations, oppression, or being in the state of "perpetual victimhood"?

"Today and beyond, let us celebrate being tuned into the True Expression of "In God We Trust" Let us be divinely intentional in our pursuit of

...Life, Liberation and Happiness!"

ANGELA SIMS-WINFREY

Just A Prayer Away...

Unconditional...without conditions or limitations

Surrender.....to relinquish control

Internal and external peace comes when we freely surrender our entire will to God. The Lord's Prayer was the first prayer I remember saying. It was the first prayer My Mother taught us and the first prayer that my sisters and I would get on our knees around the bed and say together. Our pureness and innocence did not care what it meant. We just knew that when we said our prayers, that everything would be alright. We could now sleep in comfort, security and peace. Our prayers were our nightly connection to God. Our thoughts were not developed well enough yet to "over think" or attach our "egos" to what was going to happen after the prayer. We just did it. The next morning all "the stuff" of yesterday was over and we just went about our "new day" with new adventures, new ways, and new plays. There was a purity of surrendering without conscious or condition that kept us moving forth. As we got older, we began to absorb whatever external fears of lack, limitations, and conditions we picked up on along the way. Whether it was from our parents, our siblings, family members, peer groups, our violators, or cultural environments somewhere along the way we got lost. The Lord's Prayer of our soul got "pushed down" and distorted by our fearful distractions and or detractors. It appeared that the prayers of our innocence got packed away like childhood nursery rhymes. When we stop making it our "Daily Bread", the pains and fears of yesterdays became today, and today, we feared" will most definitely be our tomorrow. Our prayer life became overwhelmed by the "etiquettes of prayer" and "how to" of what was appropriate. How we pray, where we pray and how long we should pray, what biblical verses or scriptures we use were measured by the "cliques and societal norms we attached ourselves to. If our prayers did not get answered in the time "we thought" it should be answered, we began to feel that we might not have "said it or prayed it right". Somehow we thought "we" had control over when and how our blessings or prayers should be received or answered. It became a "mental find and seek" game of delusion. Our "grown-up souls, tainted by life experiences, lost its purity of knowing that "our simple prayers" were already being handled and we can go to sleep.

What I have learned, when I "move divinely" away from the "external noise" is that God is all knowing and knows what our prayers are before we say it, whether we say it in words, song, or from our hearts. The Lord's Prayer was and will always be my prayer of comfort, of forgiveness, of request, of grace, and of mercy. As I begin to deepen my desire to grow closer to God, my "ego" attempts to "intellectualize" and stress over which prayer, which psalm, "act of contrition, or scripture was the "appropriate" one to say, depending on the circumstance. I have to confess that in my all by "myself-healing" most of the time my prayers were request for grace, blessings, and mercy for me when my back was against the wall. Knowing which prayer to say became way too ego-controlled and complicated. In my Divine Space of Understanding, I now know that God is not the author of disorder, confusion, or complication. We as "human beings" seeking control wrote many books, publish them, sold and continue to sell copies daily on disorder, despair, "who did us wrong", confusion, drama, and complication....

ANGELA SIMS-WINFREY

Our insecure ego's is attempting to distract us away from God's Divine Power within us. Seeking prayer or counsel contrary to what our "soul voice" tells us keeps us searching for anything and anyone outside of us to make us whole. What I now know is that prayer and meditation is my communion, my common union with God. Whatever prayer, biblical scripture, sermon, homily, or spiritual reading I absorb with my soul will lead me on a Divine Path of spiritual wisdom and wholeness.

In my prayer to the Lord, it is when I acknowledge that God (I am that I am) name is sacred and powerfully omnipotent. I now know that that God's Divine Kingdom is everywhere and all the blessings and lessons that have come is to fulfill a Divine Holy Will and Purpose. I am assured that the place that God's breathe life into is Heaven and Heaven is in me, through me, around me, and in everyone, and everything that I experience on Earth and beyond. I know that I am a child of God, and in the depth of pureness, I surrender my will to God's Will for wholeness. My prayers are already answered so I can rest in comfort and peace. I know for sure now that when I awake a new day is dawn and I have another opportunity to express my heart and gratitude for life and living. My sins and injuries of the past are healed and forgiven. I also know for me to have true joy and freedom in my heart, I must forgive those who have trespassed against or injured me. I know that the stronger I get in my faithfulness and devotion to God, temptation will rise higher and the journey will get rougher but I now know for sure that God's Divine Might and Power will carry me through these "rough ditches" of fear and doubt.

I unconditionally surrender to the Kingdom, the Power, the Love and Glory of God for yesterday, today, and forever.

Livin Out of Boxes...Letting Go of Bags!

It's Harvest Time!

The golden leaves of Fall are an expression of God's Greatness. IT'S HARVEST TIME! This is the time that we begin to reap the rewards of our Divine Work! Through all of the challenges we can now begin gathering up all of Life's Abundance!

Everything Is In Divine Time

For everything there is a season, and a time for every matter under the heavens.

A time for Birth, a Time for Death;

A time to Plant and a time for Harvest;

a time for Hurt, a time to Heal;

A time to Tear Down, and a time to Build Up;

a time to Grieve, and a time to Dance;

A time to Get Rid what's old, and Make Room for the new;

A time to Hug Someone, and a time to Hug Yourself;

A time to Search for what you lost, and a time to Let Go;

ANGELA SIMS-WINFREY

A time to Tear, and a time to Mend;

A time to be Quiet, and a time to Speak;

A time to Love, and a time to just Not Like;

A time for Battle, and a time for Peace!

In Reflection of Ecclesiastes 3.1

It's Time!

Livin Out of Boxes...Letting Go of Bags!

Divine Sunshine!

Oh Sunshine, my sweet sunshine shining on my face

Awakening another day

Of God Love, Mercy and Grace.

Your rays tingle my spirit, and

Penetrate my soul

Bringing energy to my body

In a new day yet to behold

Covering my body with

Its warm, comforting arms that assure

A loving embrace

That's meant to endure.

ANGELA SIMS-WINFREY

Your brilliant light reveals an essence

A Gift that keeps on giving

A lifetime of God's love lessons

As long as we are living.

Rising in the morning

Setting at night

Nurturing a purpose

That feels so right

So Sunshine my sweet Sunshine

Shine my way

Keep me glowing

In God's light and love, forever I pray.

Ashe!

Livin Out of Boxes...Letting Go of Bags!

A Rebirth: A Divine Spirit is Glowing!

So I am letting go the bags filled with pains from the past

This belongs in that time and place, not meant to last

Beyond the gifts of experiences it brought

And the Divine lessons it taught.

It's time for a healing story

That tells a bittersweet journey with all of life's glory.

A story so real, with no hidden agendas

That reveals all the pains, confusions, acceptance, and the joy of surrender.

With revelations of truth and evolved understandings

Drawing to us those who share God's Divine love for humanity

To come together as one, to heal the damage that has been done

And bring us back to a wholeness from which we all come from.

I pledge from this day forward to "live outside" of artificial boxes,

To acknowledge and take responsibility for my mistakes and actions

To strive everyday to be grateful for my blessings and lessons

To nurture God's love within me,

Spend less time with ego

Pay more attention to God Divine representative, the Will

To evolve a higher consciousness toward a divine purpose to fulfill.

To use my Time, Energy, and Attention wisely to make the world better

Fully accepting my responsibilities and taking care of God's treasures

Take care of the children he has entrusted into our care,

Leave them good examples of God's greatness, not a legacy of despair.

Free to creatively fulfill my Divine Purpose So Real

By "Being" who I Am destined to be…

…Liberated, loving, and passionately free….ME!

About the Author

Angela Sims-Winfrey, is a native of New Orleans, Louisiana. After Hurricane Katrina, she evacuated to Atlanta, Georgia where she currently lives with her son Brandon and daughter Malaikia. Angela is the CED (Community Empowerment Director) and Lead Consultant of Divine Power Transformation Network, LLC. Divine Power Transformation Network, LLC is "working net" of spiritual, anti racist , anti oppression, organizers, trainers, consultants and coaches who desire to share their Divine talents, skills, and attributes with persons, teams, families, groups or organizations willing to go through an intentional, purposeful, and empowering transformation journey.

Angela, is a Core Trainer for the People's Institute for Survival and Beyond, an internationally renown organization that conducts, *"Undoing Racism/Community Organizing*™*" workshops.* . She was also a founding Fund Advisor for the Gulf Coast Fund for Community Renewal and Ecological Health. A lifelong Community Organizer, For over 31 years, Angela gained and shared her experiences regionally, nationally, and internationally in the areas of personal, community organizing/development, personal/community empowerment, social justice, and leadership development.

Over the past 12 years, Angela designed and evolved a personal and community empowerment curriculum called, Strong Leaders: *Moving From Victims to Victors*™. The "VtoV" curriculum facilitates a healing and transformative process as a response to internalization oppression and powerlessness. *Moving from Victims to Victor*™*, Healing Paths*" are facilitated through community healing and empowerment circles. The "Healing Path" process is to facilitate participants through a journey of reclaiming strong, accountable, effective and sustainable leadership in their personal, family, and community lives.